Praise for
The Too-Busy Book

"*The Too-Busy Book* offers a compelling invitation to experience a more gentle life. Read it slowly. Read it deeply. Read it more than once. Let the beautiful wisdom of these thirty short chapters change your life."

—ALICE GRAY, coauthor of *The Worn Out Woman*

"Linda Andersen knows women. And she knows what we need. The Too-Busy Book is a practical yet lyrical invitation to lay aside the accepted chaos that seems to define womanhood today. Linda's writing is incredibly beautiful, making me hunger for a life that finds its center in the Lord rather than in my to-do list."

—JOANNA WEAVER, author of *Having a Mary Heart in a Martha World*

"Almost everyone has experienced the persistent symptoms of living an overloaded and stress-filled life. Linda Andersen delivers a potent remedy that empowers you to take control of your too-busy life and enjoy the things that matter most."

—VALORIE BURTON, author of *Listen to Your Life* and *Rich Minds, Rich Rewards*

"After reading *The Too-Busy Book,* I am convinced that Linda Andersen and I were separated at birth. Our minds think about the same things, and our hearts pound for the passion of seeing people experience the rich life that Christ made available to us. As I read each chapter, Linda took me to the place I long for—the place where I can rest without guilt, catch my breath, and soak in unhurried conversation with God and others. I am confident that the same experience awaits you. You will see it, taste it, and best of all, be given a way to get there."

> —RANDY FRAZEE, senior pastor of Pantego Bible Church and author of *Making Room for Life*

"Linda skillfully nudged me in the direction of the longing of my heart, to have more reflective and focused time to enjoy fellowship with the Lord and with my loved ones. It means slowing down my pace of life, and Linda shows how to make the choices to do just that."

> —SALLY CLARKSON, author of *The Mission of Motherhood*

the too-busy book

the too-busy book

slowing down
to catch up with life

linda andersen

WATERBROOK
PRESS

THE TOO-BUSY BOOK
PUBLISHED BY WATERBROOK PRESS
2375 Telstar Drive, Suite 160
Colorado Springs, Colorado 80920
A division of Random House, Inc.

ISBN 1-57856-742-4

Library of Congress Cataloging-in-Publication Data

Andersen, Linda, 1940–
    The too-busy book : slowing down to catch up with life / Linda
Andersen.— 1st ed.
        p. cm.
    ISBN 1-57856-742-4
    1. Christian women—Religious life. 2. Time management—Religious
aspects—Christianity. I. Title.
    BV4527.A495 2004
    242'.643—dc22

                                                        2004008949

Printed in the United States of America
2004—First Edition

10 9 8 7 6 5 4 3 2 1

《(◎)》

I dedicate this book to a gathering army of women I have yet to meet. Formidable and gutsy, these women, whom God is mustering to his side, will dare to craft their lives soulfully and live them out in joy beneath the deep-red, cross-shaped shadow of Christ. And they will pass the torch of true liberty to emerging generations.

Contents

Part III: Savor Abundance

Acknowledgments

The credit for this book can only go to the One whose idea it was in the first place—the God who yearns for us to "be" with him. While I was sitting on a park bench overlooking Lake Michigan in Frankfort, Michigan, God made known to me the extent of his desire to fill the "heart holes" in women, holes caused by too much busyness. I felt his desire to heal the wounds left by excessive activity. He ruffled my soul with his concern and asked me to do something about it. And so, because God loves and because he opened some doors, I wrote. God himself opened the first door. And the doors he opens no man can shut. To him be the honor and glory forever. Amen and amen.

Along the way, God saw fit to use my venerable editor and valued friend, Traci Mullins of Eclipse Editorial Services, to open the next door and also to sift and shift, refine and polish the presented words. And, to my delight, God also opened the door at WaterBrook Press to work again with their terrific publishing team.

As I was in the heat of writing, God opened still another

door, using Marge Darby of Holland, Michigan. Marge generously loaned me time in her beautiful little guest house. Perched high on a hill in a woods, the charming "writing hut" looked down over a creek and a family of ducks, and this hideaway was invaluable to the process of finishing the book. Marge's light was always on for me, day or night.

I also acknowledge the patience of family and friends who kept hearing about "the book."

Creation always involves the coming together of diverse parts. Thank you all for your diverse and necessary contributions. May the result you now hold in your hands fully honor its primary mover, my Father God, and be a useful tool in the transforming work he longs to do in women's hearts.

An Invitation to Live Lightly

"I don't have time. I'm too busy."

We've all heard this complaint and made it ourselves. It's acceptable, and even honorable…and so we use it. "Too busy" is rewarded in our society. So we take care to make certain we are "too busy."

I encountered this too-busy phenomenon just the other day…in a local store where I was browsing. We brushed up against each other, this woman and I. It was nearly 5:00 p.m., and the clerks told us they were ready to close. "Oh well," I said as we looked at each other over the clothes racks, "I was just killing time for about twenty minutes anyway."

Her eyebrows shot up into black arcs as she responded. "Really! I don't think I've *ever* had twenty minutes to kill."

Now it was my turn to be surprised. "*Never?* Really?"

"When you work full-time," she continued in a complaining and instructional tone as we lockstepped toward the door, "and try to take care of a family and keep up a huge lawn…" As she slid into her car, her indignant words dangled over the edge of her driver's-side window: "I just can't imagine having time to spare."

I heard both a stinging rebuke and a poignant longing in this woman's remarks. I felt chided for having twenty unscheduled minutes in my day (actually I had more than that!) and the audacity to admit it. I sensed in this woman a wistful but long-silenced sigh over the countless minutes she had seen slip away in a whirlwind. As she roared out of the lot, scurrying to her next duty, I reflected on the power of individual choice to shape and transform our lives.

Choices. Some promise freedom but instead deliver slavery. Other times, we're victims of our own good health and manifold opportunities, and we end up being eaten alive by our choices because we try to lick all the suckers at once. We usually make a choice because it appears to deliver the most benefits. Only later do we find out otherwise.

The truth is, we don't *have* to be too busy. Each of us has all the time in the world. Twenty-four hours are allotted to each of us every day. This gift of hours is ours to enjoy, to manage, and to handle with the utmost care. From the time we step out of bed in the morning until we close our eyes again at night, we all have time. The sad thing is, most of us have chosen to give it all away.

The premise of this book is that you have chosen what to do with your time, and you can still choose. Nearly everyone I have ever met has had choices she hasn't exercised—choices in favor of God's kindly direction, which will set her free. Each of us really *can* retrain ourselves to make decisions that lead to a more bountiful life: one with time not only to attend to our tasks but also to watch sunsets and take bubble baths, to share leisurely meals with friends and family, to breathe and have fun...and to pray.

This book rests solidly on the cornerstone truth that when we move closer to the root of our supposed time problem, we find that time isn't the problem at all. Choices are— our skewed choices that whip us mercilessly from one activity to another in our futile attempt to "keep up." Many of us, if not most, have said yes so many times to so many people that we find ourselves flailing around in a web, blinded to the truth that we spun the disastrous web ourselves! Moving through the essays and questions in this book will give you all kinds of ideas on how to free yourself from your sticky web—for good!

This book is about liberty. After all, the One we follow has given us freedom as our birthright. The apostle Paul scratched his head over the early believers in Galatia, asking, "What has happened to all your joy?"[1] They had been set free spiritually by following Christ but were taking back the ball-and-chain existence of trying to fulfill the Law. Christ's hard-won gift of freedom was being squandered. "Christ has set us free to live a free life," Paul told the Galatians. Emphatically he added, "So take your stand! Never again let anyone put a harness of slavery on you."[2]

As you move through this book, ask yourself, "Am I free, and am I joyful? If not, do I want to be? Will I take a stand to bring myself freedom and joy?" Because lasting changes don't usually happen overnight, give yourself permission to stroll through the chapters, pondering my thoughts while allowing your own ideas to expand and roam around unencumbered. Take your time. Don't expect too much too fast. Even if the ball is heavy and your chains chafe, you may not be willing or ready to take them off too quickly. That fact may surprise you. But your bondage is, after all, very familiar to you. And the familiar can seem comfortable even when it's constricting.

Be assured that both freedom and joy can be yours in abundance. None of us needs to live a perpetually stressed, continually overbusy life. God himself says so, and he unveils a better way. His principles for living bountifully instead of busily are scattered throughout Scripture like grain in a chicken yard. They are designed to nourish us, and they will.

But first we must acknowledge our too-busyness and admit that our efforts to handle the accompanying stress have not worked. Managing stress is a dead-end street—it takes the same old bundle of excesses, wads them up in a ball, tosses them in the air, and expects them to land in a different shape because they have been cleverly massaged.

For many of us it has been all too easy, in our headlong rush to be "relevant" and live on the "cutting edge," to stumble, tripping right over the life-giving words of Christ who calls us to another way. "Come to me," he urges. "Get away with me and you'll recover your life. I'll show you how to take a real rest. Walk with me and work with me—watch how I do it. Learn the unforced rhythms of grace. I won't lay anything heavy or ill-fitting on you. Keep company with me and you'll learn to live freely and lightly."[3]

Isn't living "freely and lightly" what we want? If it is, then stress management is not the answer. No, the key is to bore down to the core of our "time" problems so the healing can begin there. As you wander through these pages, you will discover ways to redesign and savor your life, ways that you never dreamed of and perhaps never dared to try. Choosing the path of liberty may be one of the most exciting adventures of your life!

By opening this book you have joined the growing number of people who are taking decisive steps toward changing their lives from too busy to abundant. Each essay is designed to help you first examine your own life through the lens of scriptural principles and then reshape it to conform more closely to the Master's plan. Each chapter is coffee-break length, and each is followed by questions and journaling exercises designed to prompt your own reflections and decisions. The idea is to help you stand back, take a wide-eyed look at your life now, and see what you think about changing it.

Take your time. Relax. Slow down. You have no deadline. No one cares how quickly you finish this book. There's no one behind you saying, "Hurry up!" Also, this is not a book to loan, but a personal life-change journal to treasure and keep for your own reference and enjoyment. The more time you take with it, the more you will gain. Besides, right now your life may resemble a fully loaded semi going ninety miles an hour in the fast lane. A truck like that can't stop on a dime. It needs to downshift, brake, and ease almost to a stop before it can turn a corner. And so do you.

Expect a renewed sense of delight with life when your dreams begin to slip furtively out of hiding and start to play. You may also discover that you've always longed for a few hours a week to call your own but have never done anything about it. As you read, reflect, answer the questions, and journal, you'll be unwrapping the gift of a more restful and fruitful life. Your anticipation will build. Plans will emerge cautiously from shadowy corners. You will really begin to believe that a saner pace is possible, and eventually you will be able to give yourself permission to redesign your days.

Slowing down is all about subtracting, not adding. And reading this book is not something to add to your busyness. It is a tool to help you wisely subtract and become fully focused, fully alive, and fully free to enjoy your life, your family, your world, and especially God himself.

With an open heart, then, receive this book as a gift from our God whose every thought of you is embellished with love. Discover his way of peace and abundance. Allow a new and rich satisfaction to unfold. Ask him for the courage you need to choose liberty and say no to all that keeps you from slowing down to catch up with your life.

Part I

Choose Liberty

Chapter 1

Amazed by Love

But blessed is the man who trusts in the LORD,
whose confidence is in him. He will be like a tree
planted by the water that sends out its roots by the
stream. It does not fear when heat comes; its leaves
are always green. It has no worries in a year of
drought and never fails to bear fruit.

JEREMIAH 17:7-8

"Unrealistic!"

"It'll never happen."

"You obviously don't know my life!"

These responses were coming from an audience of women hearing about the joyful possibilities of living a less stressed and more balanced life. I was the speaker, and I was not surprised. I had just made the point that life could change, and what they were saying was a knee-jerk response reflecting what they felt was truth for them—truth they just knew could never be altered.

In their remarks I heard neither willingness to change nor any hope that change was possible. And yet what they didn't say to me was as loud as their protests. I could sense that these women wanted their lives to slow down, but the courage and clarity required to change something…anything…eluded them.

They talked freely after my presentation, confiding their inability to believe in the validity of personal nurturing. It couldn't be okay for them. And so they kept their calendars filled with nurturing others. Their concern over what people would think and their fear of not having "enough" of this or that kept at arm's length a less busy and more satisfying life. The key to a well-balanced life dangled within their grasp, but reluctance and habit and fear kept them from reaching out for it. Here was a group of women wholeheartedly dedicated to hard work yet who balked at the work necessary to change their daily living patterns. *What would it take for them to change?* I wondered.

For me, it took a bout with cancer followed by years of

physical and spiritual recovery. I had time to think and pray, and God had time to change me. The day I learned I had cancer, I walked to the calendar and used a huge *X* to cross out a month's worth of activities. *That should be long enough,* I thought. After all, up to that day, I was the undisputed queen of saying yes and sure. But that began to change when the doctor stated crisply in somber tones, "Surgery…as soon as possible." I exchanged an organ for a richer, saner life. Life in the ensuing seventeen years has never been the same: It has never been so good.

Do we change only when circumstances force us to do so? I seemed to. On the very day I learned of my illness, I had just cavalierly added yet another task to my life, a task that probably would have taken me under in every way. In retrospect, I believe that God, in his lovingkindness, swooped me up and placed me carefully in the rear guard of life. No more front lines for me for a while. For long enough I had played at being in command—at being God. It turned out to be the kindest cut, this cancer. It bled, but it cleansed. The widest scar was left by God's surgery on my heart, which occurred during long walks on country roads under canopies of stars.

As I learned how to pass my days in a cocoon of restoration, the world somehow limped along without my services, and I learned that God and his kingdom could get along just fine without my assistance. He and I became tight. In my frequent times of despair, I learned who is Boss and King and, best of all, Abba…Father.

I recovered. I was changed. I would never again be so enamored with being a "mover and shaker." I had come to *know* the One who tossed the universe into space, who juggles the stars, who plays hide-and-seek with the planets. After my recovery, he left me just wounded enough to have to depend on his strength, just needy enough to never again depend only on myself. I could see, but farther now—past the end of my nose and today's list of things to do. I could hear, but finally I was tuned in to the softest whisper of his Spirit. I could walk, but not without leaning on his strong arm. The disease was my gift; its wounding, my healing. My too-busy life had looked exactly like everyone else's. But his plans for me were different—and they were good.

For months after my surgery and radiation treatment, my energy was elusive and irregular. I couldn't lean on my health. My abilities wavered. I couldn't concentrate. I couldn't plan a hot-dog roast for two! I had to say no, so I did. Misunderstandings multiplied, as in, "But you look so good!" My pride began to collapse. I had been an arrogant idiot—if I do say so myself—thinking I could be all things to all people, thinking I could do it all…and that I should. The pillars of busyness that my self-esteem rested on shook and crumbled. I now had no "work" to offer God. I could offer only myself. And I was totally surprised to find our new relationship captivating and delicious and sustaining. Day by day I learned the long-overdue lesson that my identity comes from who I am in Christ and has nothing to do with how much I produce. God loves me because he is love. *I* have nothing to do with it.

Amazing love! How can it be?

Opportunities for me to speak and write diminished. Disappeared. Only one thing was left. God alone. Would he be enough? I didn't know at first. Would I let myself receive the full embrace of his profound love for me, or after I recovered, would I keep feeding my self-importance with the husks of performance? I healed slowly. It took three years. But I was enrolled in Life 101, learning what's really important and what really matters.

Those ragged years were filled with rocking emotions, painful questionings, and hearty spiritual growth. A small green shoot of vitality began poking through the fissures in my life and taking root in the God who provides—the God who is, and who was, and who is to come. A sure-footed faith resulted because God was indeed with me when I walked through the valley of the shadow of death. Afterward, busyness no longer held such allure for me. It didn't dominate and dictate my days. Yet the smaller amount I now produced seemed to amount to more, to do more lasting good. With God more fully in my activities, they became fruitful.

"Live in me," Jesus said. "Make your home in me just as I do in you. In the same way that a branch can't bear grapes by itself but only by being joined to the vine, you can't bear fruit unless you are joined with me. I am the Vine, you are the branches. When you're joined with me and I with you, the relation intimate and organic, the harvest is sure to be abundant. Separated, you can't produce a thing."[1]

Busyness is so often mistaken for, if not actually substituted for, fruitfulness because we don't recognize the difference. "Keepin' busy?" is the first question the Dutch usually ask in Western Michigan where I live. Sure. That's easy. Busy is something anyone can be. I see busyness as perpetual motion leading occasionally ahead but mostly going nowhere, because it's unfocused, unharnessed energy. It's having the engine of our lives running at full speed in order to keep up with all we've said yes to. It's what happens when others run our lives instead of God and his good orderly direction. Busyness leaches our energy, our money, our time, and eventually our life.

In contrast, a fruitful life produces a harvest of God's goodness that spills out into people's lives. A fruitful life seems to be almost perpetually in blossom with fruit to share with others. It isn't self-focused or self-propelled. When I picture "busy," I envision a furrowed brow, tight jaw, road rage, and quarrels. Fruitful? I picture serenity (for the most part), time to spare, genuine interest in others, and a constant holding on to the hand of God. Fruitful is "busy" wearing a smile rather than a hard hat. "Busy" does too many things—things that end up harassing the soul. "Fruitful" learns to take orders from God and enjoys the replenishing interludes between his assignments.

I have learned the hard way that my role is simply to be a branch and not a self-sustaining vine. Against my muscled will I have discovered that God was so smitten with me that he pried open my fist and emptied the busyness I worshiped…in order to fill my whole being with himself. His was a relentless and tantalizing love I could not resist. I came to regard the scars of surgery—both physical and spiritual— as an imprint of a love that would not let me go.

Flooded with memories of both suffering and gratitude, I looked at the busy women scattered around the room and prayed that their own journeys from busyness to liberty would be sooner and easier than mine had been.

Prayer

Almighty God, what a wonder you are! Do you then bother to "interfere" in my plans out of love? Is this your motive? And is intimacy with me what you're after? But why? Why would you need me, want me, or even put up with me? (At times I can hardly stand to put up with myself!) Can a love so amazing really exist? I suppose that's what I really want deep down: to believe completely that the answer is yes and to experience that love to its fullest. Merely to think about a love I don't need to earn relaxes me almost instantly! Maybe it really is time to learn how to be just a branch. But I've been living in overdrive for so long. I have to think about this, Lord… Hope that's okay with you. Amen.

Reflect with Me

- In what specific ways is my life busy right now? In what ways is my life fruitful?
- Am I too busy? Why have I answered with yes, or why have I answered with no?
- In what specific ways might I become less busy and more fruitful?
- Where and when in the past might God have "interfered" in love? How did I respond?

Journal Your Feelings

- When I consider the ways I hold God's love at arm's length and try to earn it by performing, I feel…
- The thought that God loves me enough to allow pain when he deems it necessary for my development makes me feel…
- When I think about some of the steps I might take to become less busy and more fruitful, I feel…

Chapter 2

Daily Bread

*He humbled you, causing you to hunger and then
feeding you with manna…to teach you that man
does not live on bread alone but on every word that
comes from the mouth of the LORD.*

DEUTERONOMY 8:3

Spring was bursting out in South Carolina, and we were
graduating from college. Exams were over, and all of us were
exuberant. The spacious campus was happily awash with sunshine and dogwood blossoms. Romance danced in the air.
Couples in love dotted campus lawns and strolled the sidewalks, and we were giddy with seasonal joy. Our feet touched
the ground, but our heads were mostly in the clouds. We
knew we could walk on water. We were young, strong,

healthy, and armed with an impressive arsenal of knowledge that could pay our bills and transform our world. None of us questioned it: The world would not mold us—we would mold the world! What could possibly go wrong? Then came life…

It seems most of us enter our adult years with enthusiasm and a sense of anticipation. A lavish banquet of choices is spread before us, and we're eager to taste each one of them. All at once. Life! Love! Career! Success! Excitement! Adventure! Let the feasting begin! We feel strong and in control. Indeed, why should we bother a God so big and so busy? *After all,* we tend to think, *he helps those who help themselves…doesn't he?* So, with "I can do it!" as our motto, we're off to tackle the world single-handedly. And thus our race begins.

We enter the second, exhilarating lap of our lives, running headlong and happily past the mile markers of career, ministry, marriage, and children—adding as we go along. It works for a while. Time passes. Now we sprint, gasping for air, and juggle as we run. Obstacles pop up, and vicious winds threaten to send us spinning off the track. We ache with our efforts to run on dissipating fuel. Our bodies stretch and bend past capacity. Our breathing is heavy and labored.

We don't give up, but everything starts to hurt more. And we don't notice scenery along the way. Joy fades. Our flagging energy focuses solely on the race, but we keep the pace, retaining the lead outwardly but slipping inside. We're winded, stressed, and losing track of why we're running in the first place, and why we're running alone.

Enthusiasm withers, but we're too busy gathering our manna to notice. Work more. Work harder. Work longer. Work smarter. Funny, the Israelites tried it, and it didn't work. God said, "Take enough for today." But they worked longer and harder and gathered up provisions for days to come, straining past their true need. And the manna spoiled. One day's supply kept, but any more became infested with maggots.[1]

As I see it, our manna spoils too. That's why Jesus taught us to pray to the Father, "Give us each day our *daily* bread."[2] This daily provision is something to think about, to pray about. With the kind of God we have—one that offers perpetual provision—how hard *do* we need to work? How long? How much? To what ends?

I look around and see women laboring beyond reason and rationality. I see them straining to the brink of exhaustion and hanging onto the merry-go-round of life for all they're worth. But they are too busy to ask themselves, "Why am I living at this pace?" If they do look inside their souls, they see that something is profoundly wrong, but they're not sure what it is. Sermons on God the Provider are pushed neatly to the side, and these women proceed to work even more hours next week, often to "catch up." Their faith becomes unplugged from their daily life. A life-threatening disconnect occurs. And then blackout.

I think about these things as I watch the sun, majestic and sweeping, breaking through the clouds, robing the earth in molten gold, and setting my heart to music. And I decide I don't want to ever work and work and overwork on an ongoing basis. I don't want, ever, to become my own sole provider. Especially not when such a pursuit clearly violates physical and spiritual boundaries, necessary rest time, and family time. I want to work reasonably and regularly to the extent of my abilities, because that kind of work is a gift from God and provides my life with some significance. But I want God to stop me when I begin to believe I must be my own provider. I know I serve a God who doesn't expect me to live continually under a heavy yoke but instead invites me to take his easy yoke and walk in stride with him who pulls the greatest share of the load.

As a rule, I want always to take a siesta much more often than is normal in America. I want to play longer than is acceptable. I want to live lightly whether anyone understands or not. This lighthearted joy and abundance is my birthright as a child of God. I know other women won't understand it when I stroll rather than sprint, but God will. I know he wants me to work rationally and reasonably and to live more deeply than widely.

I wonder how long God has been drumming his almighty fingers on the tabletops of heaven waiting for women to relax a little and faith-it a lot? Personally, I think it's long past time for each one of us to let God bring us breakfast in bed. And I'm passionately sure it's past time to check our heart rates, slow our pace, and scoot over to make room for the God who graciously, generously, and oh-so-faithfully provides our daily bread.

Prayer

Oh, God, don't let me stand in the way of what you'd love to do for me. Help me admit my need of you and open myself to the bounty of heaven.

Don't let me set my own standard of what I need
or exchange my life for any material thing. Don't let
me be afraid to pester you each day for every need
I have. And never, ever allow me to starve inside my
tent when you've set the manna just outside. Amen.

Reflect with Me

- Do my time choices feel like a curse or a blessing?
- Do I have an hour or more each day to do whatever
  I want to, or is my life choked with obligations?
- In what ways do I routinely violate my God-ordained
  physical and mental boundaries? Do I, for example, not
  get enough sleep, eat too much food, expose myself to
  too much stimulation, or refuse myself the necessary
  downtime?
- What makes it hard for me to trust God to meet all
  my needs?

Journal Your Feelings

- When I think about God as Provider in my life,
  I feel…

- When I compare the amount of my work time to my downtime, I feel…
- When I think about working "rationally and reasonably," I feel…

Chapter 3

The Torch We Carry

There is a way that seems right to a man, but in the end it leads to death.

PROVERBS 16:25

We women don't change much from one generation to another. We only think we do. Each wave of us that comes into earth life chooses what we will and will not keep from among the ethnic traditions, faith practices, and cultural mores of our parent generation. Keep this. Toss that. We pick up the bricks handed to us by our forefathers and continue to build up and out, all the while believing that we are fresh and bright and entirely innovative in our designs, only to look over our shoulder later and find it's not so. Without wanting to (in fact, sometimes desperately not wanting to), we end up building with our parents' bricks just what they themselves had been building. It's not altogether bad that we're so remarkably influenced and guided by their values; it's just true.

Still, sorting values is a worthwhile venture. As we scrap the values that are less meaningful to us, we eventually evolve into a more authentic self. Who we are appears at last. Never content to wholly mimic our parents' way of life, each generation of women seems to lurch sharply to the left or right, ever crusading for our own beliefs and standards, eager to believe we are the first to do so, and ready to hoist flags of independence and make ambitious quests never before initiated.

Perhaps our efforts are what make the world move ahead. And we each do make a difference in our world, for better or for worse. We leave a legacy, although we seldom think about it. But the legacy is not often as profound as we wish because our dreams and aspirations are dashed or derailed or at least dulled along the way. No matter. At least we have tried and, in many ways, succeeded. And the torch will be handed off to the next generation. But isn't it important to stop and think about the torch we carry?

I've noticed that on our way to changing the world, many of us discover that the world has changed us. And when we notice that change, we're sorely taken aback. Our efforts begin to look ineffective and miniscule next to the monstrous rolling stone of our culture. At this point most of us take stock. We examine our trophies and our bruises— our badges of courage—and we say, "What now?" Do we straighten our shoulders and keep lunging in the same direction, or do we make a sharp turn in a different direction? Will we maintain the status quo? Do we still want to change more than be changed? What and who is the center of our life? And where, really, does God fit in? Are we ready to draw any new cultural lines in the sand that will minimize and even eliminate unnecessary bruises?

I have lived to see a thing, and it is this: that women of the first generation beyond the women's liberation movement have yet to challenge and redirect the overweening dictum passed on to them by their mothers' generation—that women must do it all, do it now, and do it faster. *All* includes career, marriage, children, community involvement, friendships, spirituality, personal fitness, and on it goes. The mothers of the thirtysomethings unwittingly handed to their daughters a load too great to bear, a load under which they stagger. They took it on, not knowing there was another way—not realizing that their grandmothers' lives were much simpler than theirs. And no one is saying (except in whispers) that doing it all is impossible, ridiculous—even laughable. So few, in all of society, are saying, "It can't be done" or "It shouldn't be done." A generation of women has accepted the torch without asking why—and answering why is where a shift from our chronic busyness begins.

What do I think about all this then? I will speak: *No woman can work full-time, raise children masterfully, maintain a spotless home, nurture a strong marriage, invest herself in ministry, serve in the community, and stay in top spiritual, mental, and physical shape all at the same time.* This "ideal" setup for women (note: *setup*) will never be realized.

When we allow ourselves to be set up, I wonder (if we're honest) whether our core motivation is as old as the human drama itself: I wonder if we don't want to "be like God."[1] And what is God like? Omniscient (all knowing), omnipresent (everywhere at once), omnipotent (all powerful), holy (perfect), and more.

In his book *The Purpose-Driven Life,* Rick Warren wrote:

> A barrier to total surrender is our pride (maybe that's the core problem). We don't want to admit that we're just creatures and not in charge of everything. It is the

oldest temptation: "You'll be like God!" That desire—
to have complete control—is the cause of so much
stress in our lives. Life is a struggle, but what most
people don't realize is that our struggle…is *really a
struggle to be like God!* We want to be God, and there's
no way we're going to win that struggle.

Decades ago, in *The Pursuit of God,* A. W. Tozer wrote:

We aren't God, and never will be. We are humans. It
is when we try to be God that we end up most like
Satan, who desired the same thing. We accept our
humanity intellectually, but not emotionally. When
faced with our own limitations, we react with irrita-
tion, anger, and resentment. *We want to have it all
and do it all and become upset when it doesn't happen.*

So where are the women with grace and influence, with
courage and valor, who will hoist their flags and announce,
"Enough! I'm only human!" Where are the women who will
look life in the eye and begin prayerfully and carefully choosing what must go and what must stay so that they can live
more lightly?

Every day I meet women who are designing their lives independently of God. I watch anxiously as these women's choices, even ministry choices, suck the very lifeblood from their souls and their families. Women declare, "I never sit down during the day." Taking a nap is unthinkable. Many of these women are full-time moms at home. So I ask, "Why can't you put your feet up or close your eyes for a few minutes during the day?" But false guilt and cultural pressure have produced an anxiety-ridden, compulsively busy generation of women who, more often than not, are scattered and exhausted. I recently met a woman whose idea of developing intimacy with God was to speak to him quickly while her computer booted up. God help us all.

The majority of today's Christian women have yet to effectively wrestle cultural norms to the ground and instead embrace what God wants for them: a life of serenity and fruitfulness. Where are the stout-hearted women who are ready to stand up against this rolling stone of culture? Where are the women who wholeheartedly seek after God and wisely contemplate the torch they carry? Oh, they are here. I know they are here. They are an army not yet mustered under a common flag. They may not yet be fully uniformed or trained to follow the Master, but they're on the way.

I think the day is coming soon, when women will do a holy turning back to God and back to sanity.

Prayer

Lord, she does it! And her, and her, and her! These women seem to cover every base on their own, running back and forth with no time out. But is covering the bases all that life is about? Show me just one woman who has decided to put on the brakes. I need a mentor! What? Jesus, you say? Him? Well, okay. Then let me be one you use to help change the pace at which we women live. Lord, I don't want to be a hero. I just want a life. And I think you want that for me too. I'm ready. Please transform me. Amen.

Reflect with Me

⊙ On a scale of 1 to 10 (where 1 is supremely serene and 10 is frantically frenzied), where would I rate my life measure on the serenity scale?

- What decisions brought me to where I am on the scale?
- Are there ways my life differs significantly from the too-busy culture around me? If so, how?
- In what ways do I want my life to be slower and more purposeful? What's keeping me from making the necessary changes?

Journal Your Feelings

- As I reflect on the way the culture calls me to live, I feel…
- As I think about the pressure to do it all, I realize…
- My gut response to living differently from my peers is…

Chapter 4

Uneasily Yoked

*Take my yoke upon you and learn from me, for I
am gentle and humble in heart, and you will find
rest for your souls. For my yoke is easy and my burden is light.*

MATTHEW 11:29-30

The morning flew by in a dizzying blur, as most mornings
had lately. Outside it was gray and coldly forbidding, just the
kind of Michigan winter afternoon for cozying up and staying inside.

I slipped happily into my stretchiest clothes, inserted a
favorite piano CD, and lit a blazing fire in the wood stove.
Then I curled up contentedly into the comforting arms of
my favorite chair. Beside me rested a stack of easy reading and

a steaming cup of cappuccino. Heavenly! I had given myself permission: The next hour or so was all mine. I would do nothing in particular during this time except dabble in the pleasures at hand and daydream a bit. This was sound therapy after a busy morning full of people.

Yet my thoughts wandered to the very women I had been with for a few hours. Two common threads tied our conversations together: busyness and exhaustion. In one way or another, all of us decried the busy, distracting daily rounds of our lives. After all, we were Christians whose Bibles read: "Come to me, all you who are weary and burdened, and I will give you rest."[1]

We longed for a more peaceful existence despite our careening world. "Is it really possible," we asked each other, "to slow the pace of our lives? Is there really any way to restore some sanity and serenity? Can we find a way to live a simpler life? And what, really, does being a Christian have to do with it all?" Most of the women present were tightly wound, yet we all had good health, hearty families, loving mates, and bright futures. So what was wrong?

I replayed our conversations, looking for clues. There seemed to be a number of things we trusted in: paychecks, benefits, job security, good health, government, intellect, education, relationships. What *did* God have to do with all this? More accurately, what had we allowed him to do with it?

I sipped my cappuccino and thought about Christ. As I considered his life, I saw him standing peacefully silhouetted against a brazen, bloodied backdrop of political intrigue and religious persecution. An overarching tranquillity of spirit characterized his days even though he lived them out in the raucous marketplaces and mud-spattered village streets. His was a simple, focused life: Every action pointed in one direction. His was a majestic example of controlled energy and selective restraint aimed toward the Cross. He knew what he was about, but did any of us who had been talking together that morning? Yes, we knew God loved us...but *we* had a wonderful plan for our own lives. And our plans weren't working.

I tried to read as the firelight displayed a Fourth of July finale inside the grate, but I let the book skitter to the floor. I had to admit that the yokes all of us had chosen to wear had become extremely heavy. Maybe it was time to find out what Jesus's easy yoke was all about. Maybe it was time to trade our plans for our Savior's. Maybe it was long past time for us to lead lives that left trails of peace.

Christ the Son trusted God the Father. He listened. He

followed. And he obeyed. The key to his peaceful life was that simple.

The snow had stopped falling and lay in calm drifts across the front porch. The scene was peaceful, the only sounds the crackle of dying flames and the ticking of the grandfather clock. I stirred uneasily, absently running a finger around the edge of my china cup. Empty. That was me. Busy…but empty. The time to unyoke myself from my own agenda had arrived. It was long overdue. And the process would continue for the rest of my life.

Prayer

Lord, I think I'm getting it. But how does my life transform from empty to full? And I don't mean busy-full. I'm plenty busy enough. But I'm not full. There's something missing in even my best plans for my life. So would you put your finger on it and show me how to start filling up on your agenda? I guess that's what life is really all about, isn't it? Living in such a way that I don't crowd you to the back of my bus. Father, forgive me… I didn't know what I'd been doing. Amen.

Reflect with Me

- What is the heaviest yoke I am under these days?
- If I had to describe my plan for my life up to this point, what would I say?
- What is most often the driving force behind my decisions and actions?
- For me, to really live would be…

Journal Your Feelings

- The way my life is going makes me feel…
- The possibility of improving my life makes me feel…
- When I think of what Christ said about taking his yoke upon me, I feel…

Chapter 5

A Merciful Mandate

The LORD is my shepherd, I shall not be in want.
He makes me lie down in green pastures.

PSALM 23:1-2

Jesus told his weary apostles (who didn't even have time to eat), "Come off by yourselves; let's take a break and get a little rest."[1] Similarly, a concerned friend urges, "Take a nap." An employer says, "Take a break." A doctor orders, "Take a vacation."

Are we women always going to have to be told or even made to rest? What will it take for us to take a nap, to concoct delicious interludes, to devise heart-refreshing personal time-outs—all of our own free will?

Well, I did it. Just yesterday. I spent the entire day walking in and out of stores in classy, sassy Holland, Michigan—a spic-and-span city that is a shopper's heaven. (The sidewalks are even heated from underneath to melt the snow in winter!) It was a cheerful sunny day, and I went first to the coffee shop that has tables and chairs on the sidewalk. I sipped espresso and I savored it. Then I window-shopped up one side of the street and meandered all the way down the other. Shops of every kind perched along the sidewalks like so many birds on a wire. And so I went. And so I saw. And my steps were light, my duties on hold, my joy complete as I dove into one shop and then another, filling my head with creative notions of the wildest kind. The day was brimming with satiny sun, and the hours slid through my fingers like so much sand. For me, it was a refreshing step out of the ordinary. A grouping of sabbath hours to hug to myself.

I did the same thing last week too. Took time off. We slipped away with our bikes, my husband and I, to a charming town nearby. We walked away from our duties, and we biked, and we strolled, and we shopped, and we made the very most of a golden, midsummer day which would never come again in exactly the same way. We laughed at the seagulls and admired the turn-of-the-century homes and ate delectable cuisine served high on a hill in an ancient house-turned-restaurant. I could have dusted. I can always dust. But I didn't. And I'm glad.

It's not that the concept of self-care is absent from our society. On the contrary, it's everywhere: "Simplify," "Downshift," "Take care of yourself." Armies of books with these messages line the shelves of stores. But few people seem to really be listening, and fewer seem to care about actually changing their lives. Why, I wonder, do so many women operate their lives like a tightly wound alarm clock? Why, when there is an alternative—a magnificent and merciful mandate called the fourth commandment? "Observe the Sabbath day, to keep it holy,"[2] God told his people through Moses. The Creator himself set the example for us to follow: "For in six days GOD made Heaven, Earth, and sea, and everything in them; he rested on the seventh day. Therefore GOD blessed the Sabbath day; he set it apart as a holy day."[3]

From the beginning of creation, God's hand has traced doable patterns in the sand for us to follow. After accomplishing wonder upon wonder, God took a break from his creating. He stopped in full view of the world and said, "Enough!" God—yes, the Almighty himself!—rested. (Oh, God wasn't particularly tired; rather, he was interested in modeling a way for us to live.) Later, when dealing with the people he had created and knew intimately, God lovingly commanded them to rest as well. Oh, he knew our faces would turn perpetually in the direction of productivity and performance unless we were invited, even commanded, to stop. In the gift of the weekly Sabbath, we were handed an everlasting permission slip from our Creator to turn aside from our work and turn to him in delight and worship. Every seventh day, at the minimum, we can accept the gift—receive his rest—or not.

Enter sin. Enter greed. Enter time-management seminars. Enter the term 24-7 and the lifestyle that goes with it. And enter people more interested in "making it" than "enjoying it." In my area of Western Michigan, Sunday has not completely disappeared as a day of rest and rejoicing, but in most parts of the country, people must choose to rest while the people around them don't. Across most of America the sabbath gift has been rejected—this liberating and loving mandate has been swept into a dusty corner and forgotten. I marvel that stress management is now a paid occupation. People race past life instead of strolling through it, and rest is pegged as an option only for people who want to lose the race (never mind, where's the finish line, and why are we racing anyway?). We continue to burn out and starve our souls in our race to keep up with others in the very same condition.

Sabbath implies ceasing, putting an end to activity. In simple terms, it means to turn the clock to the wall, shut off the computer, unplug, disconnect, and slip on our red dancing shoes—or soft, fluffy slippers! It means to walk away from work and allow God to use this weekly pause to reshape our souls. And if a sabbath is to do its work, only those things that refresh and refurbish should be allowed: sleeping, eating, loving, lounging, reading, strolling, listening to music, visiting, worshiping.

In *Leisure: Having Fun Is Serious Business,* Chuck Swindoll said, "There are several times we are told that Christ deliberately took a break." And consider that Jesus took his breaks in the very middle of his ministering. Even though crowds pushed and shoved around him and the sick reached out, Jesus broke away. He had a mission all right, and he accomplished it—but not in a day. Following God's timetable, he paid regular attention to his need for intimacy with his Father and rest for his body. Heaven's King in earth's armor—the Diety in a diaper—Jesus measured out his strength carefully across the years and left a legacy no thinking person can possibly ignore. Like his Father, Jesus both mandated and showed by example that we don't need to continually overwork ourselves in order to accomplish our God-given mission.

Yet we women seem to want to pack a lifetime into a day, making no room for refreshment or renewal. How many times have I heard women say things like, "I never rest from morning till night"; "When my husband gets tired, he rests. I drink more coffee"; and "Maybe if I were better organized, I could do more."

Sabbath rests are sumptuous and savory—deliriously splendid! They are Mondays in dancing shoes, Tuesdays with a cherry on top, Wednesdays with a back rub, Thursdays with a song, Fridays with a feast, and Saturdays with fireworks! They are three-layered marmalade cakes instead of yesterday's bagel. Why, then, do so few of us choose to weave succulent sabbaths into our life? I suppose that, like other directives in Scripture, we can either obey God's merciful mandate and open the gift—or hand it back and make our own ragged way through life.

Pulitzer Prize–winning author Marjorie Kinnan Rawlings wrote in *Cross Creek:* "It is better to live the life one wishes to live, and to go down with it if necessary, quite contentedly, than to live more profitably but less happily." I agree wholeheartedly. Rawlings chose to live in a dilapidated, uninsulated farmhouse in the heart of the Florida's rural marshlands and write for a living (on a manual Royal type-writer!).

I am so glad, so utterly and profoundly pleased, that at the heart of God's great plan for me is a balanced life of work and rest. Both are crucial to a joyous and fruitful life. Without work, rest would not be precious. Without rest, work makes us dull, plodding creatures.

Animals stop to rest. Birds and insects and even fish stop to rest. God's creatures don't hunt down their "daily bread" in a nonstop frenzy without pausing to enjoy life along the way. Even day dissolves into night, into rest. That's what sunsets are all about: They signal night, the daily sabbath. God writes to us through nature and signs his messages with love.

Still, rest is a choice. I can rest more regularly *if* I will. I can choose roads less traveled and arrive at a better destination. Doing so is up to me.

Prayer

Lord, this sabbath thing sounds like a dream compared to the life I live. My house and life don't look

a thing like that. In fact, Sunday is the only day
I have to _____ and _____ and _____, and
the kids always count on _____ , and my husband wants _____. Well, you know it all already!
How could I possibly take back the ground we've
lost in all our running around? Lord, would you
please help me? Would you step into this crazi-
ness and sort it out and help me think outside the
box I've gotten myself trapped in? I need a rest!
Amen.

Reflect with Me

- If God himself modeled how important it is to insert
  rest into life, why don't I do it more?

- Where, in my day or my week, could I take a sabbath?
  Why don't I do so more regularly?

- In what ways has my Sunday grown just as busy as
  other days? What one thing might I do differently to
  begin reclaiming the gift of sabbath rest?

- What can I do to make God's external commands
  into the internal "permission" to live a more restful life?

Journal Your Feelings

- When I rest before my work is finished, I feel…
- The invitation to reclaim one rest day a week in my house makes me feel…
- The changes in established routines I will need to make in order to include "little sabbaths" in my life make me feel…

Chapter 6

The Grace of Limits

*So I wouldn't get a big head, I was given the gift of
a handicap to keep me in constant touch with my
limitations.*

2 CORINTHIANS 12:7, MSG

As I see it, God lovingly gave us emotional and physical limits as boundaries to protect our health. None of us is created to do everything all the time. We have our personal stop signs. And when we continually wander past the safety zone of those God-given limits, we suffer. When we perpetually join, accept, say yes, begin, start, and add, we do so at our peril, both spiritually and physically.

But don't most of us live as if we have no limits? We watch television as if we don't need sleep. We drive as if there isn't a speed limit. We give of ourselves as though we have an endless personal supply. And we work as if there is no tomorrow. We don't consider the fact that limits are tangible reminders that we are not God but that we need God. In fact, God intentionally created us with various limitations designed to circumscribe and focus our energies. In other words, we were born unable to do everything. We just don't believe it.

In my view, limitations are a grace from God. They force us to acknowledge our finiteness and look up to his infiniteness. Our limits tell us when to stop. Even pain can be a tender mercy, announcing, "Something is wrong." Pain helps us care for ourselves. Limitations are a gift when they humble us and curb our innate belief that we can be all things to all people all the time. Even our world leaders, if they are to perform their duties, must go to bed at night and "waste" hours on sleep. Jesus himself experienced the limitations of earth life when he got thirsty and tired and hungry. He didn't do everything. Instead, with his Father's empowerment, he did what he was supposed to do. His energies were harnessed and focused.

Limits force us to focus as well. Since we can't do everything, we must choose. Every day we must choose. We must select the best action and the most important duties. We can give our full attention to those things we do choose, and the result will always be a more crafted and fruitful life.

But it is so difficult to remain intentional: to walk in a straight line without rabbit trailing! I begin one thing, and I'm pulled off to another. I start one project, and am cajoled into leaving it. I map a course only to be detoured before I even get on the bus. It's not my intention, and I don't like it, and I don't want it. But it happens anyway.

A woman's life, of course, has always been full of distractions. Fortunately, she has been programmed by God to handle a reasonable number of them with uniquely feminine finesse. I thank God he made us women with eyes in the back of our heads. I know I've needed mine. But we do have limits.

Our need for sleep is a natural boundary. Food is a must. Exercise can lengthen our days and sharpen our influence. Alone time is essential. Friendships round us out. Spousal love and family time nourish our spirits. These are basic to our happy and fruitful existence. And we are designed by God to live a celebratory life within these boundaries on which we thrive. When we shortchange our souls by denying these needs, we begin to shrivel. We eventually become small, malnourished, and unfruitful.

It is my experience that God gives us strength and grace for those things he calls us to do. But the things we choose on top of that… Well, sometimes we're on our own. We tend to live by the motto, "I *can,* so I will *do.*" After all, society tells us that doing—and the more the better—is where it's at. Multitasking is rewarded in the workplace. Double-booking is recommended. Supersizing is expected. And natural limitations are ignored or put off, and we run until we drop. Where is the wisdom in this? Where is the harnessed energy that will stretch over a lifetime instead of burning out before we turn forty? Where is the balance that gives us time to savor life along the way? Don't we privately wonder why we do everything we do? Don't we sometimes ask ourselves, "Do we really *have* to?"

It's good to regularly examine our personal limitations. It's healing to embrace the ones we can't change. And it's wise to stay alert to encroachments: the television that would rob us of a precious hour of quiet or sleep, the purchase that would snap up the limited money we have for food, the hobby that steals from family time. Even lives that are focused on doing God's work can become unbalanced. Many activities have eternal value, but does that mean God wants us to do them eternally? Not at all! Why would he have given us limited strength and caused us to need food, recreation, sleep, and so on? He will get his work done! I believe that "fruitful" happens when "busy" is held firmly in check by common-sense stewardship of our minds and bodies.

So let's stop balking at and sputtering about our personal limitations and instead gratefully acknowledge them as God's tools to restrain our wandering hearts that naturally run to excess. God knows our hearts, so he expertly shepherds us with his rod of restrictions. We would do well to heed his guidance.

Prayer

I'm sorry, Lord, but this is one of your lessons
I'm just not eager to learn. With all the pills and
potions and counseling and classes available in
America, why should I put up with any discomfort
or limitation? Downtime just doesn't mesh with my
lifestyle. What? That's exactly what you're trying to
tell me? That I need to change my life to make
room for downtime? Or else I'll hit the wall? reach

my limits? I need to think about this, Lord. Thank you for your infinite patience with me. Amen.

Reflect with Me

- What limitations has God allowed in my life?
- Am I living gracefully, thankfully, and resourcefully within these limitations? Why or why not?
- In what areas of my life do I find myself losing momentum? interest? heart?
- In what specific ways might my life change if I warehoused my energy and parceled it out more carefully?

Journal Your Feelings

- My personal limitations make me feel…
- When limits get in my way of accomplishing everything I want to do, I feel…
- If I could have one wish related to the subject of limitations, it would be…

Chapter 7

More Than Enough

*They feast on the abundance of your house; you give
them drink from your river of delights.*

PSALM 36:8

The sky is twice blue and dusted with powdery cloud wisps.
The water is a smoky Chinese silk: fair and fairer still. I watch
as gulls soar and ducks float and children toss shiny coins into
a flowing fountain. It's summer, and summer requires some
people-watching.

The summer that unwinds itself around me is slow and
measured, like the pendulum swing of a grandfather clock. It
is Eden without the snake. Waves lap against the comforting
shoulder of the shore and splash against ancient rock pilings.
Couples stroll to the heartbeat of a loving sun. A Jet Ski zips

across my view, followed quickly by the red flame of a boat slicing through the water. A tugboat chugs snail-like behind them both, and I am reminded that we need both speedboats *and* tugboats in life. But we Americans lean too far toward the speedboat side of life, victims of our own prowess in time management. We now exchange information and conduct business at the speed of sound. In fact, our love affair with speed compels us to inaccurately interpret God's directive to humankind to work the soil and ignore Christ's continual pull on our hearts to come to him and find rest.[1] We gladly adopt doctrines of efficiency as our own until we're painted into painful corners of our own making and can't find a way out. We invent ingenious ways to squeeze yet another activity into our day planners, to the point of scheduling even our loving and our play. Who would author such a life-choking delusion but the Deceiver himself?

In all our busyness and success, we have mostly failed to answer the call of God's Spirit to times of repose and reflection, to pondering and strolling and resting and abiding, to intimacy with the Lover of our souls. We have failed to truly live—to burst upon our mornings with love in our hearts and joy in our souls and energy in our bodies. But Jesus promised:

"I came so they can have real and eternal life, more and better life than they ever dreamed of."[2] And if he said it, he can do it, and I do want it, and I can have it. It is my choice to accept his gift. When I choose well, when I choose freely to do the reasonable things God requires of me, I walk in abundance—in power, in joy, in love.

But instead I have too often ridden the deceptive waves of productivity and priority planning. I've been both *in* the culture and *of* the culture, and the built-in delusions of that kind of living reached back to bite me. They wolfed down serendipity and solitude, and work became a taskmaster of the most tyrannical sort, laughing rudely in my face while driving me on.

Yes, we need both speedboats *and* tugboats. But we need more tugboats. More happy chugging, more skipping along, more fancy-free movement, and a cheerful heart; more time to watch fireflies after dark and swim at daybreak just for the fun of it.

So I will stroll more, stop often, linger longer. And I will drink deeply from the cup of abundance my heavenly Father holds to my lips. And there will be time enough. More than enough.

Prayer

Oh, Lord, help me keep my hand in yours! And
while we're on the subject, why am I so important
that you would bother? And why would you, Jesus,
leave your Father's side, sluice wetly from a womb,
and end your life on a bloody, splintered cross?
Why did you come to give me life at all, let alone
abundant life here and eternal life there? But make
no mistake, Lord. I'll take it! A hundred times over,
I'll take it. Keep me from drifting out of the quiet
places you have prepared for me, and keep me
from living a jet-ski life on tugboat energy.
Amen.

Reflect with Me

ⓒ Right now my life resembles a

___ speedboat.

___ tugboat.

ⓒ In what specific ways have I become a victim of my
own time- and stress-management skills?

◑   What personal character muscles do I need to exercise in order to make changes in the pace at which I live?

◑   Whom will I ask to pray for me during this time of transition? What specific prayer requests will I make?

Journal Your Feelings

◑   When I think of keeping my too-busy life exactly as it is, I feel…

◑   Having a person pray for me about slowing the pace of my life makes me feel…

◑   When I think about scheduling daily free time for myself, I feel…

Chapter 8

Finding Your
Sabbath Space

*"Come with me by yourselves to a quiet place and
get some rest." So they went away by themselves in
a boat to a solitary place.*

MARK 6:31-32

So where can a woman go to experience quietness? Where
can she go, at little or no cost, to attend to nothing in particular except the rhythms of nature or the play of shadows
against the grass? Where on earth can a wife, mother, daugh-
ter, executive, employee go to simply "be"—to open her heart
to God and clarify her vision? I asked myself these questions,

especially when my children were small, and I began a persistent search for places I could call my own, places where I could be nourished by planned times of personal bliss.

High on my list of requirements is ambiance. My sabbath space has to be beautiful. It needs to have a "wow" factor. I need a place where my soul can expand. If that place is a building, it must have windows that serve as eyes overlooking the beautiful. My surroundings must contain the colorful, the fragrant—several elements of the lovely. There must be something to stir my senses and color my thoughts.

Also, my place must be private—or at least secluded or apart enough to serve as a birthing suite for creative daydreaming and personal prayer. It must be a space that calls to me personally, a place where I can hear and respond to God.

As I have bent low and listened to God's still, small voice as well as to the whisperings of my own heart, he has led me to places where he has room to reform my spirit and recharge my batteries. I recommend these enchanting spaces to others who search. And in the recommending, I join hearts with the unknown author who penned these words of invitation: "You are cordially invited to attend to nothing but your peace of mind. / Leave merry this, and happy that behind. / Come, dine on hot chocolate cookies and other sweetness sublime. / Take care of this and that and the other thing another time."

Sabbath Spaces I Have Found

- a library overlooking a river
- a beach
- a car
- a path through a woodland
- my own bed
- a bike trail
- a porch swing
- a coffee shop with private booths
- a swimming pool
- an airplane
- an empty church
- a bookstore with cushy chairs
- a motel room
- a boardwalk along a river
- a city park with a pond
- my own living room, lights dimmed, with music in the background
- a bathtub with candlelight

- an outdoor reading garden next to a library
- a tearoom with vintage décor and china
- an overlook near a lake
- a bed-and-breakfast inn—for an overnight stay
- a drive through the country
- a chair and a book
- a hammock
- the base of a wonderful tree
- a friend's empty house
- a picnic table beside a river
- a public park with private benches
- a large flat rock off a mountain trail
- a chair beside a fountain in a hotel lobby

Slowing down to catch up with life begins with getting away for some quiet time—a cutaway portion of a day or an overnight retreat. Your sabbath spaces may be different from mine, but they will be food for your spirit and have the same soothing, clarifying effect. They will be places to gaze at your life and your Lord, to begin again and to reaffirm the new and slower pathway you are now choosing.

Christ was God, and he needed sabbath space. Need anything else be said?

*P*rayer

Holy Lord, this quest for sabbath spaces could be one of the most delightful aspects of slowing down. I can only imagine what it will be like to find some places of my own that are calming, nourishing, energizing. Bring some to mind right now, will you please, Lord? I can't tell you what it means to have your example to follow. You accomplished the ultimate mission with your life, but you "cut away" often and regularly. You knew instinctively that you could not be in perpetual motion. You needed rest. You needed your Father. I do too. Amen.

*R*eflect with *M*e

- Where have I experienced blissful solitude in the past?
- Where are some other places I could go to find the kind of sabbath space that's right for me?
- How soon will I go? How often can I go?
- I think I'll write—in *ink*—a couple of sabbath times a month into my schedule now.

Journal Your Feelings

- As I picture myself in my sabbath space, I feel…
- Scheduling this time for myself feels…
- When I think about explaining to others what I'm doing, I feel…

Chapter 9

On Doing and Being

And so we know and rely on the love God has for us. God is love. Whoever lives in love lives in God, and God in him.

1 JOHN 4:16

We were in the house together, little five-year-old Luke and I. My grandson was preoccupied with his play and his friends and his plans. I watched him fly from room to room, giving me an occasional glance but not really seeing me. My heart stretched toward him and yearned after him, but he was not to be won. I was aware of his presence and longed to have him stop, even for a minute, and look me in the eye and say, "I love you."

So it is with God. But our thorny and treacherous busyness keeps us away.

I have discovered, however, that change is possible. For just a short stack of minutes per day, we negligent lovers of God can embrace change. We can look up from our perpetual and incessant "doing," smile at our heavenly Father, and say something like, "How did you ever make such a beautiful sky?" And if our yearning toward him is wordless, we can merely sigh toward heaven and breathe an admiring, "Oh, God!" It is at least a beginning, like the initial stages of a courtship. First the look, then the liking, then the increased desire to be with the beloved continually.

When I'm focused on *doing* for God, the *being* with him rarely, if ever, happens. If it does, it's squeezed into the crowded corners of my life, gasping for breath. Sometimes when I'm busy performing some actual task, some visible ministry, I'm a lot like an ant swarming around an anthill with hundreds of busy others, always looking down, barely seeing beyond the task I am fiercely attending to. I lose perspective. I lose objectivity. I lose intimacy with God. My whole being is focused on "the job." I don't have the time, the mindfulness, or even the desire to stop working. At times like these, I rarely relate meaningfully to the Overseer of my work, to the Creator of my soul. I lose—and I really lose in this code-red kind of existence. When I succumb so totally to the pressure to perform, my soul shrivels, and joy walks out the back door.

God came down to the garden, and Adam walked with him. I think about this God who reaches down, who calls to our hearts, and who makes room in his almightiness for each one of us. I think about the salvation and forgiveness he provided so we can walk with him forever. Only God's grand and sweeping love can love us despite our falling so short of his ideals! And just so we could be together, so we could become one in heart! Our God yearns for each of us with an exulting and incomprehensible love—even though he probably hasn't heard us say, "I love you," or experienced a heartfelt hug from us in too long.

Doing merely completes tasks. And there's always and always yet another task to perform. Being nourishes our souls and feeds our empty hearts with the fullness of the love of God. Being. It's a taste of heaven on planet earth.

Prayer

Lord…you mean you really enjoy me…just me? You mean I'm not judged by how much work I do for you? You want me simply to allow you to love me and work through me? This is upside-down stuff to my too-busy soul. How is it that I can set

down my bulging briefcase of performance and
bring only me? Do you really… Can you possibly… And why? I'll never fully understand, Lord,
but I'm willing to be loved. I'm ready to just be.
And I'll bet it will feel heavenly. Amen.

Reflect with Me

- When was the last time I really looked up from my life,
  despite the task at hand, and simply allowed myself to
  be loved by my Creator?
- In what area(s) of my life is God showing me where
  I have lost perspective and objectivity? What caused me
  to lose it?
- If I cut back on my work-for-God hours and simply spend some of that time with him, what might
  happen?
- What might God want *for* me instead of *from* me?

Journal Your Feelings

- When I'm serving God, I feel…
- When I'm enjoying God and his creation, I feel…
- I feel closest to God when…

Chapter 10

Dying to Busyness

*I tell you the truth, unless a kernel of wheat falls to
the ground and dies, it remains only a single seed.
But if it dies, it produces many seeds.*

JOHN 12:24

In my spiritual adolescence, I am coming to know one thing
for sure: God is more deeply in love with me than I will ever
comprehend. Immanuel: God with us. In love with me. And
in love with you.

A twin thought scoots in beside the first, adding: He
wants the *best* kind of life for us, his beloved ones. A world-
class life. Blue-ribbon living. Spirits set free and continually
rising like kites above and beyond the fuzziness and muddi-
ness of life. His plans for me and you are always good. He is
better to us than we can ever be to ourselves.

Yet another thought (a triplet?) pushes in between the first two, and it is this: The hard times, the pain, the detours we take—all are continually gathered up by our Father God and transformed into chariots of grace to us. God is always cleaning up after us and sending us on our way forward. This is no new truth—only a restatement of what God speaks throughout the Bible. He is continually redeeming you and me from sins and brokenness and stupid mistakes—making us new in spite of our many faux pas. We fall down. He picks us up.

This threefold truth, braided together, becomes the strongest rope imaginable. It enables us to rappel confidently over the edge of our too-busy, too-constricted lives, and embrace the adventure of choosing liberty.

There's another truth I find to be a reliable guide, and it goes like this: Life seems to be a continual repetition of three things: (1) crucifixion/death; (2) burial; (3) resurrection. Think with me because this pattern does relate to our over-busyness.

Something in our life is always dying or about to die. Youth. Love for a person or an activity. Passions. Desires. Plans. Hopes. Opportunities. The work we do.

Consequently, something in our life is always being buried. We seem to always be putting something behind us—a cherished plan, a sorrow, a tragedy, an addiction, a memory, a highly anticipated event. We learn to let go and move on.

Thankfully, then, life is full of resurrections. Something new is always about to begin. Maybe an old love or interest resurfaces, or new vitality bursts out in our spirit or our church. The liberating truth of this reality is that we are never stuck. There is an open tomb. When the stone is rolled away, things can change. Actually, they do change, whether we like it or not. But we can proactively initiate good change in our lives. And we are not alone. God wants to help us bury busyness and birth a life that has sparkle and dash.

I know about deaths and resurrections because they have happened to me. I once came to a desert place in my writing, for instance: a place of dryness, parched words, sour spirit, and sore woundedness. I was fallow and unable to breathe life into my shriveled words. So in one wrenching moment of total surrender, I let my writing die, believing it would be gone forever. I turned to something completely different and began to create one-of-a-kind note cards with my hands. When I slipped free of the compulsion to write, renewed creativity began to trickle in slowly through a completely different tributary. I didn't know it was happening. I had just given myself a sabbath. Instead of demanding that the same kind and the same amount of energy flow through me continually, I relaxed. In time, I was once more compelled to write—and the words came like a river. I learned in retrospect that even during the supposed death of my writing, life was being incubated. I was becoming revitalized. God's resurrection power was quietly at work in my circumstances. But renewal happened only because I allowed something to die. The whole cycle was necessary: life, death, burial, resurrection.

These cycles of nature have always delivered fine sermons, but I've only just begun to hear them. Consider the sermon of my apple trees. They preach from the side yard. In May, blossoms spring forth, flamboyant and promising. Then they appear to die and drop off. For a time nothing is seen, but suddenly tiny new buds appear. More time passes, and life is harnessed in the buds, which eventually burst into apples. Then with winter comes an enforced sabbath for the orchard. Nothing appears to be happening. Yet life is being created and stored in the stalwart womb of each tree. In the right time, when spring breezes fondle the leaves and the sun romances its branches, the orchard blossoms again.

If we would take notice, the cycle occurs in nature *and* in life. If you're a woman desiring to birth a different kind of life, there is indisputable hope! In the womb of our waiting and wondering about what to do, a new vitality is burgeoning. The seeming death of our current way of life becomes the birthing room for new life to come. In God's hands, our winter of the soul becomes a holy gestation period that delivers a life laced with space and peace and laughter and love and time to spare.

I think of Jesus, and I'm instructed. Christ himself didn't really want to die if there was another way to redeem us. But he went all the way to the Cross. And for a while, all appeared lost. Yet in his death, a life-giving power was incubated which would stretch from Genesis to Revelation, and would embrace you and me centuries later. There really is a right time for things to die, and they must die to make way for new life.

The way most of us American women live—perpetually adding, accumulating, speeding up, squeezing in—nothing dies. We constantly figure out how to cope instead of change. We make it work. Fit it in. Wind it tightly. Move it quickly. We have no time to change. None. Not for God's sake. Not for ours. Not now. Not yet. Slowing down just isn't done. We don't often insert commas and colons in our lives, only in our writing. Siesta is for someone else. We believe each day must be lived at high velocity or we will fall behind (behind what?). We become virtual robots of busyness until our batteries begin to leak. And then we replace them right away so we can keep on going. But when our lives go on and on without regard for the natural rhythms of the seasons, without sabbaths to gestate new life, isn't it inevitable that we crash and burn? And isn't the very crashing and burning simply evidence of a body and spirit insisting on attention?

In my opinion, when we humans ignore the foundational patterns of all creation (life, death, burial, resurrection), we gain nothing, no matter how fast we work or how much we accomplish. An unrelenting and too-busy pace always brings the same result: a burned-out body and soul, which will find a way to rest—even if it's in a hospital bed. I think even some depressions can be traced to an overwrought soul deciding to take a leave of absence from the race. So we best heed the muffled screaming inside us that says, *Wake up! Let the madness you've accepted as normal die, and allow God to resurrect your courage to live lightly and well.* A loving God won't give in to the pounding rhythms we've decreed; he will keep urging us to die to the pace that has become normal.

To stop a life that is spinning out of control and declare war on it is a profound act of courage. Life will never be the same. And it will never be so rich. To pronounce the death penalty on busyness and roll back the stone of fruitfulness is definitely reason to celebrate!

In the words of the apostle Paul, I know I am called to be crucified with Christ and yet live![1] My God keeps exercising his divine authority, pulling me to himself and pointing me to the cross where something must die and be buried. He also points to the kernel of corn that must die in order to live and produce a harvest. I try every way possible to resist, but when I finally do nail my stubborn and resistant busyness to the cross, I find my God raising me from the living dead.

Our arrogant sin of busyness can and should be laid at the foot of the cross. After all, you and I are like three-year-olds insisting we can tie our own shoes. We need to hand them to our Father, and when we do, he covers our hands with his and shows us how.

Even so, Lord, tie my shoes.

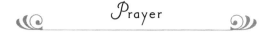

Prayer

Lord of heaven and earth…Lord of me…I have a sense that something in my life is about to die.

Something is about to change forever, to change
for the better. Right here, in the whirlwind of my
chaos, I can feel the gusts of change. My life has
been spinning in this too-busy pattern for so long
that it's out of breath. And so am I. I guess if nothing changes, nothing will change. So I'm ready to
let this too-busy way of living die. To tell the truth,
I desperately want it to die. I'm sick of it. But I
need you to step in and help me bury this too-busy
life I'm living. I don't think I can do it on my own.
Oh, I got here by myself, I know, but I really don't
want to keep trying to tie my own shoelaces anymore. Amen.

Reflect with Me

- Under what circumstances is God's love for me most
  evident?
- What are some of the things in my life that need to die?
  How will I know when it's time?
- In what areas of my life am I still trying to tie my own
  shoes? What one small step can I take toward giving the
  shoelaces to God?

◑ What would I most like to see come to life that has been dead too long?

Journal Your Feelings

◑ When I consider the idea that being too busy has its roots in sinful arrogance, I feel…

◑ When I imagine giving God my shoelaces, I feel…

◑ When I think about _____ coming alive in my life again, I feel…

Chapter 11

Traveling Lightly

All the days of the oppressed are wretched, but the cheerful heart has a continual feast.

PROVERBS 15:15

The cavernous airport terminal throbbed with life in the fast lane. Monotonous voices droned from every speaker, and frigid air washed in and out of automatic doors in shivery waves. Caterpillar lines formed at each gate, and cell phones popped in and out of pockets like so many prairie dogs on a summer day.

Flights were cancelled. Schedules were changed. Eyebrows arched, and the soul of the building was filled with the mournful voices of the delayed. It was winter in Michigan.

I watched as the caterpillar rearranged itself after each

announcement. Boxes, bags, purses, golf gear. People lurched and surged with their burden—now in line, now out. Lines disappeared, and people stood in forlorn groups, wondering what to do with their time—and their baggage. Various options, none of them easy. Pack it. Stash it. Carry it. Fold it. Drop it. Push it. Roll it. Stow it. Hundreds of passengers faithfully lugged their treasured possessions behind them yet appeared to desperately want to be rid of them.

But one traveler was different. This one, with skin of ebony and eyes sparkling with good humor, apparently had no baggage. He alone stood happily in line and then moved happily out of line. He beheld the solemn and dour mien of those in line and decided, this one with no baggage, to do something about it.

Mostly he used his wide smile. Wrapping itself around him and stretching beyond him, it touched several people who were close. They, too, began to smile. They kept on smiling until, one by one, person by person, the caterpillar line was one long, unbridled smile. It was a gift from him who had no baggage.

Then the laughter caught on too. He laughed and he laughed. He laughed at himself and at his plight. He laughed so deeply that his belly shook. First one stranded passenger, then another, found his laughter irresistible. They laughed together. And because the laughter lingered in their hearts, they kept laughing as they left one line for another. The elfin man was helping them with their baggage. In his freedom he lifted their boxes and held their wraps. The man with the empty arms became a hat tree, a closet, a bellboy. He couldn't have done so if his own arms had been full of heavy burdens. If he had been limping and lurching through the caterpillar line trying to care for his own stuff, he probably would not have smiled, much less laughed. And there would have been no one to help carry so many others' burdens.

The man packed lightly. The man traveled lightly. The man probably lived lightly. And his hearty laughter transformed an airport terminal. His shared joy reset stuck spirits.

Later, travelers at my gate jostled their way onto the plane, stowing their goods, mumbling complaints under their breath and groaning their dissatisfaction. Only a short ride away from the gate, we stopped again. And then a two-hour delay on the runway. Tempers flared and children cried. The smallish man with the empty arms began talking. And again he smiled. He laughed some more, and he told stories. Once more his contagious good cheer wound in and around and among the passengers until it had done its work. His laughter bounced over and beyond his seat, working its jolly way around the cabin.

He had no baggage. He carried the people. He shouldered their loads and bade them smile. In a blizzard, in the middle of winter, in the overcrowded cabin of an airliner, I saw the Christ at work. I saw liberty incarnate.

Prayer

That's me, Lord. I stand in line for something all the time. And I'm loaded to the rafters with stuff I think I need. And it's not just physical stuff either. You and I both know the clutter I seem to draw into my life. And the load is getting me down. Oh, dear Jesus, reach down and lift this burden of busyness and too-muchness. Rescue me from myself. Teach me to travel lightly. Amen.

Reflect with Me

⊙   What are some of the things and circumstances weighing me down?

- If Jesus's burden for us is light, where did my heavy load come from?
- Which of my burdens can I do something about right away? Which ones can I set down, shift, or leave behind?
- Am I living my life lightly enough—are my arms empty enough—that I can help carry another person's load when God asks me to?

Journal Your Feelings

- When I stand outside myself and look at the load I am carrying, I feel…
- When I imagine my life as slower and lighter, I feel…
- When I consider setting down or getting rid of the burdens of _____ and _____, I feel…

Part II

Redesign Your Life

Chapter 12

Holy Stirrings

Today, if you hear his voice, do not harden your hearts.

HEBREWS 4:7

When I think about how changes in my own life begin, I see that discomfort is usually the scratchy, awkward beginning—the first peckings of change. I begin to stir uneasily in my shell, where some baby-bird part of me has been incubating, getting ready to emerge.

For any of us, the stirring begins in the heart—where God meets us in secret. Suddenly the status quo no longer satisfies. The world's—or even our own—"good enough" is no longer good enough. Life seems tarnished, tattered at the corners. God seems to be reaching out for our reluctant hand

and drawing us toward change. We are intrigued but afraid. We pull back into our shell where we know exactly what to expect. But the stirrings return, and again we risk some movement. We cautiously peck at our shell until a wide crack reveals boundless skies outside.

For most of us, personal growth is uninvited and generally unwelcome. At least it is for me. My life today is, as a whole, balanced, serene, and fruitful. But it hasn't always been. At one point, my yeses had put handcuffs on every hour of every day and had thrown away the key. I was bound and gagged by my own choices and by my nagging need to be viewed as important and worthy. It took a health crisis to set me free. And a map. And a guide. God was there. I already knew I was too busy to experience the abundant life he offered. Only he knew it would take a bout with cancer, a brush with death, to teach me how to stop being the victim of my own choices.

I believe the stirring to change is present inside every one of us whose life keeps bumping into itself at the corners and whose activities keep us stuck in fast forward. So we women must listen to our stirrings! We simply must. They sometimes begin with nothing more than a wish and a sigh, and we wonder, *How can we retrench? How we can restore some bal-*

ance and sanity to our lives? Recognizing our stirring becomes a desire. This longing catches fire and becomes a fervent prayer: *What do you want me to do, Lord? How can I slow down my life, Lord? I'm listening.* Our thoughts begin to reposition themselves as we listen to the voice of God. And our life begins to turn a corner.

After the *will* comes the *way.* But what exactly is the way to a slower-paced life? What did Christ mean when he said, "I am the way, the truth, and the life"?[1] How does one act on the sacred desire for a slowed-down life? What can we do to grow an invisible yearning into a visible life transformation?

I believe we must begin by discussing our listless longings and garbled wishes with the God of love who declares himself irrevocably on our side. If we wish for a more tranquil life, we must begin by laying our tangled lives down at the scarred feet of the One who listens and intervenes. Then we must humbly admit our inability to untangle the knot we have created. At this point of surrender, God's omnipotent power surges in, and our hands intertwine with the explosive, creative hands of the Divine. There! We find ourselves on the threshold of a new beginning. We have joined forces with the God of heaven himself.

Once we have acknowledged our need for change and

linked arms with God, we are able to begin looking objectively at each slice of our lives: the occupational, social, spiritual, recreational, marital. Where are we out of balance? We start to see where we've overdrawn our time accounts and where we're paying dearly in crunched days and flagging energy. We begin negotiations in earnest: *What can I do, specifically, to change this, Lord?* When we're finally open, God can do outstanding and surprising soul work.

I love the words of ancient devotional master and church father Jean-Pierre de Caussade: "God is not making an impossible demand on you. He is only asking that your good intentions be united to His so that He may lead, guide, and reward you accordingly." He adds, "Those with good intentions, therefore, have nothing to fear. They can only fall under the almighty hand which guides and supports them in all their shortcomings; which leads them towards the goal from which they are straying."

I've experienced how hard it is to stop life in the middle of the street when the light is still green. The traffic behind you is in the *go* mode, and everyone is honking! Stopping at that moment is a daring feat. It declares to those around you that green is not the only color in life. There's also yellow. There's even red! But it takes resolve to stop running the red lights in our lives and begin heeding life's and the Lord's cautions. Yet reevaluating our direction and our pace right in the middle of our journey boldly announces to our souls that, in a life well lived, *slow* and *stop* have as much value as *go*.

Prayer

Holy God of the universe, I'm amazed that you have time for me! That you are interested in my tiny life and actually care whether or not I'm too busy! But according to your Word, you care profoundly. And I am choosing to take you at your word. Lord, I absolutely am going too fast, and sometimes I lose my way altogether. I don't know where to turn but to you. Here I am—what's left of me. Please help me design a life that reflects your values. I'm so glad you have all the time in the world. Amen.

Reflect with Me

What peckings of change within do I feel these days? I will identify several ways this stirring of change is manifesting itself. Are they pleasant? unpleasant?

- In what ways does my life seem tarnished or tattered at the corners?
- I will ask God to join me in looking objectively at various slices of my life: the occupational, social, spiritual, recreational, marital, and so on. In what areas am I out of balance?
- Have I ever done anything *permanent* to slow down and redesign my life? Why or why not?

Journal Your Feelings

- When I wake up in the morning, I usually feel…
- By 10:00 p.m. I often feel…
- When I think about huddling with God and renegotiating my life, I feel…

Follow Your Heart

Trust in the LORD with all your heart and lean not on your own understanding; in all your ways acknowledge him, and he will make your paths straight.

PROVERBS 3:5-6

When it comes to finding direction in life, I am discovering that each of us needs to trust our own, God-enlightened sense of "right" and "ought" regardless of what anyone else may think. Others will always think they know what we should be doing, saying, or thinking. But only One knows the heart, because he made it. Only One completely understands us. Only One will listen to everything we say without interrupting or prejudging.

So why do so many of us flail around in confusion inside a web other people have spun for us? Why do we walk through doors someone else has opened? Why do we sometimes chart a course we don't even like? Why do we listen intently to the opinions of others and all but ignore the voice inside us? If we are walking with the Lord as closely as we know how and inviting his input into our lives, then why isn't that enough to motivate change? Why, since he will faithfully guide us by the counsel of godly companions, the Bible, and even circumstances, do we let his voice be drowned out or diluted by the voices of others?

Someone—and sometimes many someones—will have a plan for my life and for yours. Advice is free for the asking, and plenty comes unsolicited as well. This advice can conflict, and it often grates on us and confuses what we know deep down to be true. But usually, if we stop long enough and often enough to pray and meditate, study Scripture, and listen for God to speak to us, we will have the only plumb line we need for decision making. And his voice will not contradict his Word or ask us to do wrong or add burdens we can't bear. A good and valid test of whether God is speaking is the peace that follows. His peace accompanies his directives even when they seem difficult to follow.

There will be times when God's call on our hearts will be misunderstood by others and difficult for us to explain. Few people in my life, for example, have ever fully understood that being a writer is a real job requiring time, regularity, solitude, and a thick slice of personal discipline. At a time when I was writing three or four full days a week, plus caring for three children, a husband, and a home, an acquaintance asked seriously, "Have you ever thought of getting a *real* job?" Working from my home has never been understood. Surely I can go here and there at will or talk on the phone whenever it rings or stop whatever I'm doing for someone who wants something. After all, I'm not really working.

A friend of mine and passionate follower of Christ, Pat Bos, found herself being called away from visible, measurable service for God into the invisible, immeasurable ministry of intercessory prayer. God intimated to her that she would be criticized, misunderstood, and harshly judged by some, but his voice was clear. And so she began to change her world and ours by her obedience, which continues today. She can explain to only a few, and has stopped expecting people to understand why she doesn't serve in a more common and visible way. She is following God's pointed and unique call, and she contains it with joy in her heart.

I like that. There's power in such spiritual focus. There's a rightness in saying yes to a single commander, the heavenly Commander-in-Chief. Showers of spiritual energy are released into our world by this kind of focused containment. This isn't trying to water a field with a small pitcher.

I think about Mary, the teenaged mother of Christ. The angel said, "You will give birth to the very Son of God, Mary. Your womb will carry a Savior." Mary pondered these words in her wise and discreet heart, realizing that God's plan for her life would cast a holy and a permanent shadow over her own designs. But she willingly laid aside all of her dreams. She heard God's call, thought it over, and obeyed wholeheartedly. And that single-hearted devotion drew sharp misunderstanding from her friends, neighbors, and family.

Mary's life was an arrow pointing clearly in one direction. If my life and yours are going to be arrows pointing to God—if we are to walk strong in the direction of our dreams and God's callings—we'll need to hold our heads high through tall weeds, looking straight ahead and listening to only one voice: his. We'll need to lay aside every weight that bogs us down, that busies up our lives, so we can run the race which the God of the universe has marked out specifically for each one of us.

Sometimes, when every dream, every plan, and every call of God is laid open to the curious inspection of well-meaning people, God's direction can get stepped on, side-tracked, or lost. We don't have to share everything in our hearts with people—especially if the sharing will mean loss. There may be a right time and a right person with whom to share our cherished dreams and visions, but not everyone who applies qualifies. People don't need to understand. God already does.

Prayer

Lord God, I'm so tired of sweeping my heart and your voice under the proverbial rug. Sometimes I think I hear you speaking a direction to me, but when it doesn't match what others expect, I just pretend I didn't hear you. No wonder I've run into some glitches along the way. Father, I want to listen to you more closely and then obediently take the road you assign—even if at times I must travel without others. Your voice in my heart is reliable. Empower me to follow it. Amen.

Reflect with Me

- Which of my life choices seem to be understood, even applauded, by others? Which choices seem to be misunderstood and sometimes even criticized?

- Who in my life is advising me and offering direction? Is that input solicited? unsolicited? What words best describe their "help"?

- Is my prayer time a one-way street, or do I listen for God's voice in quiet meditation? What might make me a better listener?

- In what specific ways might my life be different if I followed my heart?

Journal Your Feelings

- When people offer unsolicited advice about my life's design, I feel…

- When I follow others' advice for my life against my own better judgment, I feel…

- When I reclaim personal responsibility for myself and trust the Bible and my God-enlightened heart for direction, I feel…

Chapter 14

Reroute and Recover

But as for me and my household, we will serve the LORD.

JOSHUA 24:15

Six-year-old Brendin DeVisser walked into his kitchen, dirty from head to toe, with a praying mantis on his head. He was grinning from ear to ear and couldn't wait to share his joy. I was there with his wise mother, Sue, who had decided not to run him from camp to swimming lessons to sleepovers to Vacation Bible Schools to birthday parties during this one summer. "He's too busy playing with grasshoppers," she told the many who requested her son's time. And Brendin grew tall and brown and strong and vitally connected to the natural world around him. He flourished.

fe today looks a lot like a board game. Pick a
_____ a move. Ten steps forward, eight back. Your turn.
Now mine. Back to home. Start again. Not much changes
from day to day except the pace—and that keeps accelerat-
ing. We run to keep up, but we fall behind anyway. Why can't
we stop running? Because, privately, we're afraid of not keeping up. Sometimes we run just because we want to. Or perhaps we feel overwhelmed by the sheer number of our
options. So many places to go and so many things to do! We
have to run in order to do it all.

But how can children look for bugs if they are standing
in line at a theme park? In *Celebration of Simplicity,* Richard
Foster speaks eloquently of the "too-much-ness and too-
many-ness" of our world and urges a civilized restraint of our
desires. He believes, as do I, that our hands are too full of
candy and there's not enough time to eat it.

Families often run forward at lightning speed, passing
through crowds of people also in running shoes, people who
cope by lengthening their stride, increasing their pace, or
stretching work and "activity" hours while reducing downtime. There is an unspoken but palpable fear of losing this
endless race that actually has no definable end. Yet another

deep-down "knowing" is also frightening: Keeping up is a thief. It steals the spontaneity and joy of living, and it saps the vitality of family life. It ignores the basic human need for open space where we can stretch out our thoughts and hear ourselves breathe. Sometimes kids just need to lie on their backs in the grass and daydream. (So do we!) But keeping up makes us clones of a harried culture already floundering in its own excesses. We literally forget how to slow down because we don't get enough practice.

When we look closely at the average family's time problems, we can see how they developed in the first place. It becomes quite obvious that personal choice has had everything to do with how busy families are. In most cases, families have simply made choices that subtract from family intimacy and add unnecessary busyness. But the good news is that we can all return to rational, good-sense living by taking the same road we arrived on: the path of personal choice. Simply put, there's no way to slow down except to put on the brakes and shift into reverse: We need to decide what to eliminate because eliminate we must. That's how we get unbusy and open up space for being fruitful. As Christians, we are not called to merely manage stress. Rather, we are to extinguish stress—to banish it and reinvent a family life that slams the door in the face of excessive busyness. Our call is to follow Christ so closely that as he directs our paths, we feel the dust from his sandals on our faces.

To follow Jesus in this way, families will need to say no many times a week to a lot of people. If we have a higher purpose for family life than busyness, saying no will get us there. One mom I know kept track of a single day's requests for her time outside the home. She also estimated the hours each yes would have meant. The eight requests would have added forty hours to her already full days!

Saying no is a parent's priceless gift to the family unit. It's too easy for parents to lose direction and take their hands off the wheel of family life, letting it drift in neutral, or worse, career off the road. But saying no puts us back into the driver's seat so that we can guide the family with wisdom and love. Such a small tool—saying no—but it's one that will determine a family's destiny and legacy.

There is a best road for any family to take, and even if the family has veered to the right or left or run off the road entirely, it can get on that better path. God can redeem the lost time, and the family, together, can once again know purpose and joy.

Prayer

Lord, my family and I are on a runaway horse, and there's no stopping it! Or is there? I wish I could see more clearly. What exactly do you want us to change? What I wouldn't give for some free nights at home—some wide-open spaces on my calendar and my family's. Some weeks it seems that we hardly see each other, much less spend quality time together. But here I am sounding like a helpless victim! Lord, you say that all things are possible with you. You know what? I'm ready for us to jump off this wild horse and tame our lives. Please catch us, Lord, won't you? Amen.

Reflect with Me

- Which societal values does our home life reflect? In what ways does our home life reflect biblical values?
- What can I do to eliminate stress in my home? in our family life?
- From whom am I most likely to encounter opposition

to slowing down, to my efforts to design a more satisfying and fruitful family life?

❧ What simple, one-sentence version of no can I use
to courageously carve out more time for my family
to enjoy life and each other?

Journal Your Feelings

❧ When I imagine having more unstructured time in
our home, I feel…

❧ The idea of bringing up this whole too-busy issue with
my family and discussing it together makes me feel…

❧ Having more time together and more opportunities
to foster intimacy with my family members makes me
feel…

Chapter 15

Saying No

*God wants us to grow up, to know the whole truth
and tell it in love—like Christ in everything. We
take our lead from Christ, who is the source of
everything we do.*

EPHESIANS 4:15, MSG

I sat in a group of educated, middle-class, thirtysomething
Christian women as they chatted about simplifying their
lives. Several said that they couldn't possibly say no to even a
phone call, that they had to answer it each time it rang.
Others talked uneasily about wanting to say no to some
people's demands and intrusions but not having the courage
to do so. The desire was there, but the willingness was not. I
saw that at the root of their discontent, they simply didn't

believe in the validity of their own desires, plans, goals. And disbelief ate up their courage.

Saying no may be one of the hardest but best things we women can ever learn to do. It's hard because we feel so ever-lastingly guilty when we say it. A replay button seems to go off each time we do manage the *n* word, and it goes something like this: *You shouldn't have said that. You know you can do it. You should do it. There's no one else to do it. What's wrong with you anyway?*

We humans like to be known as ready, willing, and able, and we revel in being known as doers. Oh, yes, it is more than hard to say no. But until desire partners with our will and takes action, we are destined to remain victims of others' agendas and pawns of our culture, which seems to exclusively reward our yes.

And that point brings us back to the matter of choice. Do we or do we not have choices in our lives? Yes! We do! We're not puppets on God's strings—or on anyone else's. We are creatures made in God's image, made with a free will. We have the almost frightening power of decision.

In my own life I have too often helped others fulfill their life purpose to the exclusion of fulfilling God's call on mine. And this compromise always turned out wrong. *To the exclu-*

sion is the key. When any of us drifts *always and only* in the direction of others' wishes, we lose sight of our own road. We start merely reacting to life rather than initiating good things. God's unique purpose for us gets fuzzy and sometimes lost altogether. Christ understood this tendency, so he set his mind and will on his mission and walked deliberately face-forward toward the Cross, undeterred by efforts of the Twelve to crown him then and there. I love the example he set.

What, then, should we say no to? To everything that hinders the primary calling on our life. There are reasonable exceptions, of course, but those will be plain and usually unavoidable. And they're usually temporary. We all make exceptions, but the general direction of our lives can resume when the crisis is resolved.

"Everything is permissible for me," the apostle Paul told the early Christians at Corinth, "but not everything is beneficial."[1] *No* is a premier sorting device between the good and the best, like the pickle conveyor belt in my hometown. All the pickles are dumped onto the conveyor belt: big, small, and in between. Along the way, a sorting device allows the oversized and undersized pickles to drop through slats. The device says yes to the best pickles and no to less than the best. Just like us. We all have various choices to sort through every day. With one misplaced yes, we can find ourselves over-loaded and underenergized for our primary, God-ordained tasks. So sorting is a must for Christians, because we want our time and our life to really count for our Father's purposes.

Take today. I must say no to answering the phone and to taking a walk this morning (it can be done later) in order to write (my primary calling). One call could mean forty-five minutes on the phone. I must choose or lose. Saying no in this case captures necessary time for God's particular call on my life.

Or take last week. I was invited to a party at an acquain-tance's home, a party that would take both hours and money I didn't have to spare. I declined, explaining, "I rarely attend par-ties, but thanks so much for thinking of me." My no was hon-est—and I gained hours. I also clarified the relationship and avoided future invitations. Over the long haul, such simple decisions to say no may have opened up months of time in my life to attend to the primary things God calls me to do.

In fact, deciding what is most important makes it easier to say no to the less important. I love my Day-a-Month Away With God (DAWG Day). It helps me keep my life in bal-ance. I go to the lovely wicker-strewn porch of a friend who works away from home during the day, and God and I begin sifting. I tell him what I'm doing, he asks, "Why?" and I have to answer. I always come home rearranged and focused and energized.

Each life, it seems to me, is a flowing river in danger of draining away entirely in tiny driblets. We can easily drift aimlessly in the direction of others' plans for us, always facilitating their plans and not respecting God's plans for us. The willingness to say no is a powerful conduit of life energy, worthy of harnessing and using. Saying no will make us God pleasers more than people pleasers. God's call is doable and enjoyable because he equips us for it. Man's call is usually hard—a hard yoke and a heavy burden.

Saying no is difficult because it's so final. It's clear, and it seems almost rude. But we can decline opportunities gracefully, thanking the one who suggested or offered: "I appreciate your confidence in me"; "I'm sorry, but that just won't work for me right now"; or "I wish I could, but it's just not possible." There are ways to soften the blow.

Saying no may well be the most powerful and most valuable tool in a woman's toolbox. The word *no* cuts an impressive swath through the tangled jungle of choices and distractions of today's world. It is a gleaming sword of courage! When sharpened, it has the ability to positively alter and improve our life direction every day. When wisely applied to our decisions, saying no reserves our energies for the best actions instead of the lesser or even the harmful ones.

Used well and often, the word *no* is preventive medicine. It keeps us from overinvolvement and inferior decisions that wound our lives. Better than aspirin, *no* does away with the headache even before it begins. Saying no gives us white space on our calendars and a sense of guided freedom. It gives us time to step outside and look at the stars or watch a sunrise or read a book on a porch swing or go for a spontaneous bike ride or take ourselves to lunch.

Life is God's sweet gift to us. It is not to be continually or thoughtlessly squandered on the less important, but lived out fully within the context of the most important.

Prayer

I don't know about all this, Lord. It sounds so
simple, but you and I both know it isn't easy.
Maybe it's possible, though, at least to a degree.
I'm sure saying no has to be practiced a lot before it
becomes easier. I'm also sure that being able to say

no would make me feel like my busyness doesn't have to remain like a car without the brakes. When I keep saying yes and getting into collisions, I don't respect myself for allowing it. Truthfully, Lord, most of the time my yeses are a kind of lie because they don't speak the truth—the no—that's trying to squirm out of my heart. I guess all I can say for now is, please help me. Show me how to use this no tool in a considerate and wise way. Show me how doing so will help set the right balance between diligence and spontaneity. Ride with me on the wings of this new practice, because I do choose to fly in this direction. Amen.

Reflect with Me

- When do I feel most powerless to say no?
- What's behind my reluctance to say no?
- My life isn't exactly the way I'd dreamed it would be. What are some initial steps I could take toward creating that life?
- How might the kingdom of God benefit from a few, well-chosen noes from me?

Journal Your Feelings

- When I say no to anybody about anything, I feel…
- When I don't say no and I know I should, I feel…
- When I consider the ways my life could change if I learned how to say no skillfully and gracefully, I feel…

Chapter 16

Why Not Ask Why?

They are a nation without sense, there is no discernment in them. If only they were wise and would understand this and discern what their end will be!

DEUTERONOMY 32:28-29

Ask why about doing almost anything in America, and you're sure to draw stares. Nevertheless, *why* is one of my favorite questions, but it doesn't necessarily make me a favorite in discussion groups. Why? Because it's disturbing to be asked why we do something. It makes us uncomfortable. We squirm as it forces us to minutely examine the motives behind our actions. It insists we submit our intentions and desires and plans to personal interrogation and push them through a refining grid before mindlessly proceeding.

Asking why also takes time—time we don't have.

Asking why looks tradition and habit boldly in the eye and questions their validity, opening the door for a fresh wind to blow through. The why question also challenges the encrusted status quo by suggesting sometimes that we go left instead of right. It says, "Why not this instead of that?" or "Why not no instead of yes?" It doesn't even hear, "We've always done it this way."

For most of us, why is a big, malevolent burr in the saddle because it stops us cold in our tracks and requires from us deeper, more probing thought before we proceed. We all find it easier to say, "Whatever works." We don't find it as easy to scrutinize our decisions and involvements. Basically, why is an uninvited stop sign in our personal fast lane. We just don't like to ask the question.

Yet I firmly believe that why is a gift to a too-busy person. It provides us with a one-word grid to sift our choices. "Join us!" "Be there!" "Do this!" "Give here!" Cries of need and discontent daily overwhelm our ears, jostling and cajoling for our time and beggaring our resources. It's easy to cave in either for lack of fortitude to refuse or for lack of energy to ask why and think about the consequences. It's also easier to act than to pray and ask God's opinion about our considered purchase, action, or commitment. But for the woman who is ready to make positive changes that will lighten her life load, asking why may be her all-time best friend—her junk sorter, her caution light—insisting that she think before she acts.

Consider a child who wants an expensive pair of shoes because "everyone else has them." Ask why that is or isn't a legitimate reason. Does this purchase stand up to the scriptural principle of good stewardship of the finances God has given us? What about the spiritual principle of denying ourselves? Will the purchase keep us from giving to others as Christ has given to us? Will buying these shoes for the child strengthen or weaken her character? Will it require his parents to work more, thus taking them away from quality time with the child himself? Has God provided the money? Has anyone prayed about the purchase? See how the tiny word *why* is a helper—even with a pair of shoes! It provides a purposeful pause, a semicolon, a buffer zone, a time-out to think through the repercussions of both yes and no. Because there are repercussions to both, and they're worth considering.

Life is not so valueless a commodity that it can be frittered away. This is especially true for believers whose lives are an extension of heaven on earth. We're Christ's ambassadors, his personal representatives, carriers of his light. We show who he is to those around us. We bear the telltale marks of his crucifixion in our lives. We have the delightful privilege of sharing his love with a love-starved world. And, in the light of all the work to be done, we must make careful, prayerful choices.

Clearly, because asking why reveals our motives, it helps us make better choices. It is, however, unquestionably dangerous—often personally uncomfortable and wildly in opposition to our cultural programming. But, carefully employed, asking why can be the key to a life that sizzles with energy instead of sagging under the weight of too much.

Prayer

My Father, you live in heaven. I live on earth. I want your kingdom to be evident down here like it is up there. Please give me only what I need to help make that happen. Forgive my sins and help me to forgive other people in the same way. Please don't let me get near temptation, but pull me out before I get too close. Teach me how to ask why about my activities and to answer with bold discernment. Because the way I live my one life—your sacred gift to me—is on the line here. Not to mention the reputation of your kingdom, your power, and your glory. Please help me be a good steward of this life. Amen.

Reflect with Me

- What parts of my life do I need to thoughtfully push through the why grid?
- What makes me hold on so tightly to certain parts of my life? In what area(s) do I feel the strongest (internal and external) resistance to change?
- In what ways might some of the choices I make, almost unconsciously, be affecting my availability to God and my usefulness for his kingdom purposes?
- How might asking why before I make a decision bring some sizzle into my daily life?

Journal Your Feelings

- When I think about interrogating myself and scrutinizing my motives, I feel...

- When I consider praying carefully about even the smallest decisions, I feel…
- When I picture the reaction of friends, coworkers, and family to my whys, it makes me feel…

Chapter 17

On Adding

*So do not worry, saying, "What shall we eat?" or
"What shall we drink?" or "What shall we wear?"
For the pagans run after all these things, and your
heavenly Father knows that you need them. But
seek first his kingdom and his righteousness, and all
these things will be given to you as well.*

MATTHEW 6:31-33

Somehow, every time I add to my life, I end up subtracting
from it. Whether things, people, or activities, these additions
never fail to disturb, reshuffle, and rearrange the terrain of my
life. After all, now there's something more to engage my
attention, drain my energy, and slice into my hammock time.
So unless I subtract something that is equivalent to each

thing I add, I diminish the quality of my life in at least a small way. Each addition will cost something. So the question must be, Is the addition worth the cost?

When I add something, I must take ownership and responsibility for it. If I add stuff, more time is chopped out of my days. Life becomes a bit more complicated, more full of care. That new thing calls for my attention every time I pass by. It becomes yet another item I must do. And it begins to own me, to dictate how busy I am, how much money I need, and how much I need to work.

Cars. Houses. Land. Furniture. Clothes. Clubs. Sports. Second jobs. It's the old story told by each succeeding generation—keeping up with the Joneses. And I have to ask: "Is that thing or activity worth it?" Well, sometimes, it definitely is. Sometimes I truly need this or that. Sometimes God plainly wants me to buy or join or participate. But isn't there a point at which I'm better off when I stop adding? Simply stop? Isn't there a time to draw a line in the sand and say, "No more!" And doesn't that need to happen well on this side of burning out? The trick is tuning in to the voice in my soul that's saying, *Enough.*

But then, where possessions are concerned, I must battle with my economic prosperity and my own innate delight in accumulating. I must, to be frank, do battle with the lust of my eyes, the lust of my flesh, and the pride of life. Shades of Eden![1] Eve wanted; I want. The battle began in the garden, and it still rages fiercely inside us today. A victory, then a loss. A loss, then a victory. Perhaps decisions about material things are more easily made in poverty than in riches…in sickness than in health. In poverty we humans discover quickly what is important and what will last. In sickness, priorities are easy to see and act on. I must eat. I must rest. I need to recover. And so I focus on those basic needs of survival.

But how, in this country of abounding wealth and continual excess, can I hope to control the tidal surge to have more and do still more? Will I ever learn to experience deep and daily satisfaction with what I already have? What can I do to fend off the lust for more of everything? Can I ever, by the meaty and satisfying grace of God, stop climbing and even step off of the ladder of continual additions?

For me, and I think for all Christ-followers, the answer is, I can't. At least not by myself. Not completely or for all time. I'm not capable of being anything beyond a covetous child who wants and wants and wants some more. But then, there is God. And he is near. And he longs to transform my warped and wanton desires. So I name them, I ask for him to intervene, and by his power I let them go. For only God—the God who made me—can ever put his finger on the primal source of my relentless wanting, cauterize it, and over time, heal it.

For my part, I can keep my eyes from sights that ignite scorching desires…and my feet from malls that set me up for failure. I can spend more time appreciating and enjoying what I have instead of searching for more. I can do those things. I can also stand in front of the mirror of my life and practice saying no to nonessential, perpetual activity and even to unnecessary "people time" (socializing). I can avoid invasions that significantly hinder my primary purpose of living each day as an act of worship.

But will I? The choice is mine.

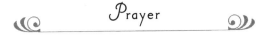

Prayer

Dear God, it's me again. Do you know what I've just realized? I've seen that my constant urges for more are just blatant admissions that you are not enough! Please…take charge of my slippery steps and my vagabond heart. Show me what you want me to add to my life—and what I'll need to subtract when I do. Show me clearly what I merely want to add but don't need to add. Honestly, Lord, please turn the light on because I'm as good as blind sometimes. But you already know that. Thank you for being willing to illuminate my path. Open my eyes where I am blind and push me in directions you choose. Amen.

Reflect with Me

- In what one area can I practice not adding any more?
- In what ways do I window-shop and expose myself to temptation? Do I, for example, glance through catalogs, read magazines, watch television, frequent favorite stores, and so on?
- What can I do to reduce my spending instead of trying to earn more? And what commitments do I need to eliminate instead of adding more?
- In what specific area(s) of my life can I trace my sense that I have to overwork/overdo to the core sin of coveting (wanting what I don't have)?

Journal Your Feelings

- When I browse through catalogs, stroll through malls, or Internet shop, I feel…
- When I think about sorting and selling or giving away some of my possessions, I feel…
- When I consider cutting back on people time, specific activities, or certain ministries, I feel…

Chapter 18

On Subtracting

Whoever tries to keep his life will lose it, and whoever loses his life will preserve it.

LUKE 17:33

One cool summer evening, a friend and I relaxed by a crackling fire in a cute, tucked-away cabin. We both wanted to look at our lives with an eye toward simplifying and slowing down. My friend listed on paper the activities she was involved in, including raising a family, and realized there weren't enough hours in the day to do all she had committed to do. This realization was a step toward balance for her, a step toward clearer focus that brought her rich fruitfulness in a couple of involvements instead of minimal fruitfulness from scattered busywork.

In *It's Only Too Late if You Don't Start Now,* Barbara Sher wrote, "A quality life has a lot more to do with what you remove from your life than what you add to it." Centuries earlier Meister Eckhart wrote, "Only the hand that erases can write the true thing." I couldn't agree more. If we want to slow down to catch up with life, we will begin by subtracting.

I think of my friend Karen Weaver. She mothered two children and gave quality attention to her husband. Her smallish home was pleasing and pretty yet obviously lived in. She didn't have a car when everyone else did, and she took time for walks in the country. Her manner was calm; her spirit serene. Her duties left her pleasantly tired but not stressed. She modeled a life that so many other woman wanted but weren't really willing to have.

When I asked Karen to tell me her secret of living such a simple yet fruitful life, she said in characteristic humility, "I can't speak for what anyone else should do, but my husband and I just try not to do too much or own too much." I was taken aback. *That's it?* That sounded too simple. And yet, as I thought about it, it actually sounded too hard. None of us naturally leans toward "losing our life," laying aside our agenda, truly emptying ourselves in order to make room for God's plans for us.

When I think of obvious things to subtract from my life, several items come to mind: too much food, too many possessions, too much house, too much yard, too many clothes, too many cars, too many activities, too many projects at the same time... Personally, I love to throw stuff out. It's easy and fun for me. I get a thrill from cleaning out, sorting, giving away, and tossing. I always have empty cupboards and shelves. But it's not so easy for me to do the same with my projects or activities. Or people! Through the years, God has made my primary mission clear to me, and it is encouraging women. But even on this I can spend too much time, and the result is an unbalanced life.

I—we—would do better to ask, "How much (of anything) is enough?" And, even more important, "How much of this did I choose, and how much did God choose for me?" We have become persuaded, sometimes even by well-meaning preaching, that adding to life is the only choice we have. But perhaps closer to the truth is that it feels like adding is the only choice we can make without guilt in our society—and even in our churches. The push is always to do more and get more.

I'm convinced by Scripture as well as experience that God does not require us to be so busy at work or ministry that we live under a continual time crunch and feel stressed most of our waking moments. That leaves only two other sources behind the pressure to be too busy: ourselves and others. I think, to a large degree, we make the decisions that end up making life too busy—and we get plenty of "help" from even our most well-meaning friends and relatives. In some cases, our very warm-heartedness has gotten the best of us, and we have added beyond what we can or even should try to be managing. But we are so used to the weight of the loads we have chosen that we seldom consider subtracting from them. We hardly feel the weight anymore. We've forgotten what it's like to live lightly. Because we have choices, we tend to put more on our plates. And if our plate looks full, we think organizing the contents is the answer. So we organize better and free up more time. Then we get busy and add again. And organize again. And the insane cycle continues.

Let's face it. Every container, including people, has a limit. Every glass has a point at which it's full. Every ship limits its cargo. Everything in life—even a sponge—can hold only so much. And when that saturation point has been reached, there's a reckless and uncontrolled overflow. But what if the full point is never reached? What if one teaspoonful of water is removed for every one put in? Then the glass would never get past full. Perhaps then when we overflowed, it would be with the joy of a full cup rather than with the careless gushing of a too-full life spilling out indiscriminately.

Prayer

Lord, I wonder what would happen if I eliminated one activity or thing or obligation for each one I took in. If I subtracted something every time I added—or subtracted just because!—the world probably wouldn't fall apart. So please show me where to start. You and I both know what my glass of life looks like. I need your wisdom to know what to subtract—and when and how. The book of James says that if we lack wisdom, we should ask you for it. Well, I'm asking. And I'll be listening for your answers. Amen.

Reflect with Me

- If my life were poured into a glass, what would that glass look like?

- What are some logical candidates for subtraction from my space or my life? Which payments? activities? social events? chores? television watching? mindless Internet surfing?
- Why does it take courage and discipline to subtract from life?
- If I don't start subtracting now, what is likely to happen?

Journal Your Feelings

- To consider having my life look different than other people's lives makes me feel...
- Thinking about a woman who lives as Karen lives makes me feel...
- When I think of the life I really want to live compared to the life I'm living, I feel...

Chapter 19

To Do and to Don't

*I am the resurrection and the life. He who believes
in me will live, even though he dies; and whoever
lives and believes in me will never die.*

JOHN 11:25

Epitaphs fascinate me. They always have. How can a person's life be scooped up in a sentence and carved on a stone? "She Never Gave Up." "Beloved Father." "Blessed Little Lamb." Some of these people lived eighty or more years, and their legacy in this tiny graveyard was a sentence—a pithy synopsis of their personal "dash between the dates."

A crisp October breeze laughed its way through multi-colored treetops as I scuffed along through layers of fallen leaves littering the ground. This cemetery was near my home, providing me with an easy place to go and think about life. Someone had carefully mowed around each gravestone for the last time this season. His work was neat and precise. As clouds scattered in all directions, buffeted by strong autumn winds, I reluctantly acknowledged that winter was waiting in the wings and fall was about to leave center stage.

Jamming my hands into my pockets to keep them warm, I wondered about the life represented by each gray stone. Each person had made decisions that took her somewhere. Stooping to brush away a cobweb from one marker, I knelt in the crunchy leaves beside the grave of a woman who had been a mother. Surely she had been busy. All mothers are. Surely she had made choices in order to create room for her child. All mothers do. I then pondered the importance of the things we women do, and the things we don't. I considered how the way we spend our hours determines the legacy we leave—our final fingerprint. I thought of the steppingstone decisions made every day that determine a life. There are dos and don'ts, choices we get to make, choices freely granted us by our Creator.

Reaching for the scratch pad and pen I always keep in my jacket pocket, I began jotting down a few dos and don'ts that had helped me sift through all the choices. The lists below, which took fuller form over time and changed through the years and the stages of life, have served me well as a blueprint for a well-balanced life.

Dos

- Decide the seven most important categories to spend your time on. My list looks like this (in order of importance): God, family, home care, ministering to others, personal renewal, occupational interests, and friends. Keep this in mind: "But seek *first* his kingdom and his righteousness, and all these things will be given to you as well."[1]
- Do one thing at a time. Enjoy each step instead of hurrying on to the next one.
- Do turn the phone ringer off when I don't want to be interrupted.
- Do maintain more times of quiet in our home. Make a "silent night" party of it.
- Do say no a lot more than is ordinary or "acceptable."
- Do find ways to live within the income God provides.

- Do keep open space in every day, every week, every month, every year—for emergencies, personal time, the unexpected.
- Do always claim my gift of Sunday rest as a sabbath gift from God.

Don'ts

- Don't mindlessly believe I "need" something because "everyone else has it."
- Don't be continually available to anyone (including husband and kids) except God.
- Don't do too much, and don't own too much.
- Don't forget the joy of having white space on the calendar!
- Don't cave in to others' whims out of cowardice or passivity.
- Don't plan activities back to back with no space in between.
- Don't put on a heavy yoke when Christ wants to give me a light one.
- Don't give ground to those who don't understand my choices.

Slanting rays of afternoon sun scissored through the tree-tops, turning the leaf-covered grass into a carpet of gold. Rusty brown leaves still clung to the strong arms of the giant oaks rustling like starched petticoats in a Civil War movie. A sudden, cooling breeze whipped across the grass and stirred the sleeping pine trees. Time that afternoon had moved on. Even here where time stood still.

The cemetery visit had energized yet cautioned me. Each life was a gift to be opened only once. And I wanted to keep unwrapping mine wisely and well.

Prayer

Oh, Lord, please look at my life with me. I want to leave a really good legacy…one that will show by example your wise and winsome ways to live. But if that is going to happen, I need to make some U-turns and midcourse adjustments. Show me exactly what to do and what not to do. I'm listening. I'll even write it down. Amen.

Reflect with Me

- What do I want inscribed on my tombstone?
- What legacy do I want to leave?
- What message is my life sending now?
- Which of the dos and don'ts above might be good ones to put on my own lists?

Journal Your Feelings

- When I think of having a specific blueprint for living, I feel…
- When I'm at a funeral, I feel…
- When I'm old and looking back over my years on this earth, I want to feel _____ about the life I've lived. For that to happen, I'm going to have to…

Chapter 20

Devotions on a Rock

*Foxes have holes and birds of the air have nests, but
the Son of Man has no place to lay his head.*

MATTHEW 8:20

Today I bought a nice chair. Not a big chair and, as chairs go, not an expensive one. Twenty-five dollars and I was out the door. A bargain for sure! And I can rarely resist a bargain. Today I didn't even try.

It's not as if I was hunting for the little chair. The chair found me. At least that's how I like to tell the story. I was simply nosing around at an outdoor antique place with some extra money jingling in my purse when I saw it: small and golden and posing comfortably in the crooked doorway of a tumble-down barn. There was a kind of halo around it. And it looked lonesome. It was fairly clean, custom-made, comfortably upholstered, and exactly the right size for my devotional corner. Ah—a "holy" justification!

I instantly loved the chair and convinced myself that I needed it. So I bought it and then pushed and shoved until it fit into the trunk of my car, neat and tidy and protected against the Michigan road slush. It was an orphan no more.

But now the chair stares me down. It sits on the screened-in porch because it needs a little work. It looks out of place, but it needs to be shampooed before it can be carried upstairs. Still, it is the perfect color. And it is the perfect size. And I did have the money. So why do I feel uncomfortable?

Well, if the truth be told, I didn't really need the chair. And that's true about a lot of things I now own. I already have places to go for quiet time with God. I could have used the money elsewhere or on someone else. Now I have to make a special trip to buy upholstery shampoo. And I have to find time to clean the chair, to carry it upstairs, and then someday to move it or otherwise dispose of it. And if I don't, my relatives will after I'm gone. The chair is mine, for better or for worse, for richer or for poorer, in sickness and in health. It has squeezed its way into my life, and there's no turning back.

So just where do I stop with this consumption? At what point do we believers stop? Maybe the stop sign is already written on our hearts, and we simply drive through it without thinking, much less slowing down. Maybe we need to allow God to police our hearts on even the little things lest the Deceiver use them to trick us into believing it doesn't matter where we go, what we do, or what we bring home. But it does! Because little by little we find ourselves encumbered. Suddenly we're using too much time to care for too much stuff. This accumulation sneaks up on us! Of course it does.

Oh, the little chair is sweet, and I do like it, but today it's talking to me about caution and prayer and restraint. It glistened there in the golden rays of the afternoon sun. It shimmered from the doorway of that faded barn. It called out to me, and I was gladly wooed into "just a little purchase."

But now…what about my friend whose husband deserted her and left her on her own to fight cancer and raise a child? They could have eaten for a week on my twenty-five dollars. And what about the couple who can't pay the rent this month because of an injustice? Am I my brother's keeper? Yes, but I shirk the job. I justify my choices, and I try not to look around because then I might really see the sin of my greedy gathering when other believers in my circle don't have enough.

But the chair did speak to me—and it called louder than the truth. It worked its way into my devotional corner, and now it's mine. And the twenty-five dollars is in the hands of someone who probably doesn't need it as much as other people I know do.

Then I think of Jesus and how he lived. I think of him, but I don't want to. No house, no closet, no boat. No devotional corner. No yellow chair. And I wonder: Couldn't I have my devotions on a rock?

Prayer

Oh boy, Lord, I'm thinking about how fast I complicate my life. Too often when I see something and want it, I spring into action. I just get it. What do you make of that? Help me think it through, Lord. If I changed this greedy pattern of mine, I would need less money. That could mean less work…and more time to spare. Why do I do this, Lord? What is this shadow lurking in my heart that keeps me busy earning money in order to feed my habit? You have your work cut out for you: changing me. But something tells me you're up to the job…and I'm glad! Amen.

Reflect with Me

- What is the first thing I think of doing when I have a little extra money?
- How did I rationalize my recent spontaneous purchases?
- When was the last time my excess supplied someone's need?
- In what ways does my desire to acquire make me too busy? What can I do to start changing this pattern?

Journal Your Feelings

- When I buy something I don't really need, I feel…
- My first feeling when I become aware of someone else's financial need is…
- When I think of how Jesus lived his earthly life, I feel…

Chapter 21

Saying Yes

Simply let your "Yes" be "Yes," and your "No,"
"No."

MATTHEW 5:37

I know a woman, a good woman, who works with great devotion in the ministry she's been called to. But too often she chooses to follow her own need to perform, and her positive involvements turn on her. They rob her marriage, deplete her strength, and steal her joy. She rarely closes out her day in a comfortable tiredness, able to transition smoothly into a restful evening with loved ones. Instead she keeps on working. All those watching her know the pace cannot last, because she is not saying yes to God's gift of a well-rounded, enjoyable life.

Saying yes is a favorite habit of the woman who always feels too busy. "Sure," she says, "I can do that. It's no problem." Or, "Why not?" We have a thousand ways of saying yes, and lots of reasons for doing so. For one thing, yes gets people off our backs. It makes us feel omnipotent. It boosts our self-esteem (temporarily). It keeps us from being bored. It saves us from having to be purposeful about what we choose to do. And it flatters our ego because we're needed and viewed as capable.

But saying yes for these reasons is usually self-defeating. Why? Well, people come back and ask again. And we quickly discover we're not all-powerful after all. We come smack up against our limitations and feel the pain. We may not be bored, but we're doing something uninteresting to us, and we're doing it without conviction. We beat ourselves up because we didn't have the courage to say no. Or maybe we just got uncomfortable saying no and wanted to try a little yes on for size.

There's nothing inherently wrong with saying yes. The trick is to use yes in a positive way—a way that builds our life instead of tearing it down. I like to think of yes as a big, wide, welcoming front door to my life. A "come on in" kind of thing. Yes invites someone or something to enter our lives.

We become a host to that new activity, job, or involvement with its demands on our time and energy. We might even need to eliminate or reshuffle current involvements to make room for new ones. Push. Squeeze. Shove. Adjust. Will the sacrifice be worth it?

Maybe we need to ask, right up front: *Will this yes help me fulfill God's purposes for me, or not? Is it a logical step or am I going to get sidetracked?* The wisest man in the Old Testament urges us: "Let your eyes look straight ahead, fix your gaze directly before you. Make level paths for your feet and take only ways that are firm. Do not swerve to the right or the left; keep your foot from evil."[1] This sounds like intentional living to me.

Opening our lives to good involvements, fellowship with godly people, and balanced work is certainly within the scope of God's plan for our earth life. And yes can help be our "chooser." Just as saying no closes doors and keeps us from fruitless sidetracking, a well-timed yes opens doors to abundance and purpose.

Because we live in this land of multiple choices for everything from coffees to cars, our choosing muscles need to be strengthened and toned. So we need some kind of practical exercise to work out our choosing skills. For years I have used the following set of twenty questions when I reach a decision point and need to say yes or no.

1. Have I waited twenty-four hours before answering?
2. Have I asked God for wisdom and direction?
3. What is the motive behind my saying yes or no?
4. Does my spouse (or family) agree with my viewpoint? Are we in harmony?
5. Do I have the passion to see the commitment through to completion?
6. Do I have the ability to do what I'm being asked to do?
7. Would my efforts duplicate someone else's?
8. Is there a simpler, more creative solution than my saying yes?
9. Can I do this with a cooperative, uncomplaining attitude?
10. Will a yes subtract from my family life significantly and/or for a long period?
11. Will a yes sidetrack or derail my personal mission or vocation?
12. Do I honestly want to do it?
13. Do I have the required amount of time set aside or available?

14. Would I be squeezing this commitment into an already too-full life?
15. Do I have the physical stamina I need to do the job?
16. Do I have the money in hand, or would I need to go in debt if I said yes?
17. Will compulsion, desire, or God's call determine whether or not I join or attend this?
18. What is my gut-level, common-sense, best judgment in the matter?
19. Have I sought the counsel of my mate or a trusted mentor?
20. Do I have complete peace about my answer? (Lack of peace is a red flag.)

There are stacks of yeses we could choose from that will lead to fruitful living. Say yes to health time. Say yes to marriage time. Say yes to children time. Say yes to God time. Say yes to playtime. Say yes to friend time. Say yes to work time. These yeses are all necessary and welcome pieces of our lives, and they keep us moving purposefully down the track in good directions. But when our yeses start taking us down sidetracks, it's easy to get completely derailed.

Both no and yes help keep our energy fine-tuned and our lives moving full-steam ahead. Our freedom to choose is a great gift. Let's commit to saying yes and no with the confidence that comes only as a result of asking Christ to be our Conductor.

Prayer

Where are you, Lord? Still there, I hope, because I'm counting on you to be my life's Conductor. You see, I don't do well at figuring out when to say yes and when to say no. That's how I got in the mess I'm in now. I really need your wisdom. Please show me how to use my yeses more purposefully, to bring some order and good direction to this sometimes derailed life of mine. I want to say yes with confidence, and I'm going to begin by saying yes to you more often. Come on in, Lord! Fully inhabit me. You are welcome here. Amen.

Reflect with Me

- To what or whom do I say yes most often? Why?
- To what or whom do I have the most trouble saying yes? Why?

◌ Which area of my life seems to be chugging full-steam ahead in the right direction? How can I tell?

◌ Which of the twenty questions seem to trip me up most often? What can I do to change that?

Journal Your Feelings

◌ When I consider saying yes right now to someone or something that requires an answer, I feel…

◌ When I say yes to an involvement I'm not sure I'm equipped for, I feel…

◌ Saying yes to things and people who nurture and strengthen me feels…

Part III

Savor Abundance

Chapter 22

Retreat

As the deer pants for streams of water, so my soul
pants for you, O God. My soul thirsts for God, for
the living God. When can I go and meet with God?

PSALM 42:1-2

Ah, retreat! The very word relaxes me like the sound of a
bubbling brook. It satisfies me like ice cream on a hot day,
and warms my soul like a hot bath on a cold day. The word
retreat has always brought Frankfort, Michigan, to mind.
This sleepy little hamlet nestles happily along the sugary
beaches of Lake Michigan in the northern part of our state.
Frankfort is everything a small town ought to be—and then
some. We've gone there all our lives, my family and I. When
life got too busy or too heavy, we went as a family. When our

marriage needed fluffing up, Roy and I went. When summer was just too gorgeous to resist, we jumped in the car and headed north.

I've also gone to Frankfort alone. Two or three times a year I go. I steal away and head north to a delectable lakeside hideaway, and whether I stay two days or only a few hours, I feel like a new person. The little old tourist home I stay in is charming and safe. Run by a cordial and hospitable couple, this storybook place sits snugly between the house next door and the Frankfort Hotel. It's today with all the charm of yesterday. I am received like a favorite relative, and my privacy is respected. Breakfast is quietly delivered to my door at 9:00 a.m. and covered tastefully with a pretty linen napkin. And there I am, enjoying breakfast in bed! A perfect excuse to linger over prayer, reading, quiet reflections.

Frankfort yawns and stretches its way into every languorous morning. Nothing opens until ten o'clock, and then business slowly wakes up. People stop in the middle of the street to catch up on news. Cars mostly amble along. Salespeople are friendly and genuine. Shopkeepers carry their coffee to the sidewalk and visit with one another, while a dog or a cat lies sleeping in their open doorway. Somehow, the pace reflects the way things ought to be. I can feel it in my bones.

On my busiest days I replay these images of Frankfort. And before I start becoming an enemy, even to myself, I call and reserve a night—sometimes two. Oh, holy privilege! Oh, dire necessity! For the price of a new dress, I restore my soul.

My drive north is just the beginning of this retreat. I pray, I rest, I listen to music, I lose myself in the watercolor splashes of the season around me. And I begin to find whatever part of me gets lost when I'm too busy. It has been that way lately, so I go. For two nights I go. I will not be sorry.

The first day is a kind of exhaling—a giving away of worries and demands that push and pull at my days, often contorting them into scratchy garments I don't want to wear anymore. On the second day I begin to breathe in—to receive from God and to be nurtured by the lavish natural beauty all around me. Sleeping late is part of my retreat. Propped in a charming bed, all mine, my body can unfurl slowly and meet the morning naturally, like the sun. With the world white-shuttered out and embraced as I am by my cottagey room, my thoughts can stretch out, go new places, wander endlessly. I can get lavishly lost in daydreams without any interference.

I listen for the noises of the morning as the village yawns its sleepy way into this yellow summer day. I think yawning is one of God's delightful designs, nudging the body both to sleep and to awaken. A yawn is a halfway moment between rest and activity, a signal for preparation, a green light to go to bed—or to get out of it.

"I can't go to bed till I've yawned," proclaims Aubrey, the child of my child. She is a knowing creature, fully alive to the joys of being awake, yet responsive to nature's call to rest. She is small. And she is never stressed. Her little life is never over-done. She never has too much on her plate (unless some grownup puts it there!). Fully a child, she plays through her day, sleeps when she's tired, gets up when she wakens, laughs when she's tickled, and cries loudly when she's hurt. She even stomps her foot when she's angry. No inhibitions here! Fully attuned to the rhythms God wired inside her, she bounces happily into her days and rests soundly through her nights.

O child! O woman! O me! What has happened to thee? Where have you gone? What have you done that you fight rest when you're tired and you wake up only when an alarm jangles? In the beginning it was not so. Whose voice did you hear when you chose a hundred destinations and arrived at none? What cunning deceit lures you over and over again to fill your boat so full that it overflows and threatens to sink?

The cadence of a calmer life speaks to me. And this

retreat helps me hearken once more to its voice. For my God has not made me to overdo—not consistently, not for too long, and not without rest. Even in music, in a symphony, there are rests. If there were not, the raw notes would razor against each other, muffling the singular notes and obscuring the melody. So it is in life.

From Scripture I know that the Lord has made provision for his children to have a joyful and abundant life. If I ignore his achievable plan and overfill my vessel, I have been the causer of and the reason for my pain, not him. For the most part, I choose both what and who goes into my boat. And I remember a truth God teaches: that he will not command us without also enabling us. So if I am stressed by too much activity, I think it may be a sure sign that I am my own black-caped villain.

The God of my life is also the redeemer (thank goodness) of all my frailties and failures. I think he must always be about the job of putting me and my Humpty-Dumpty life back together. Always, and always, he is the buyer-back of my assorted troubles and stupidities. By his own admission, he is busy about the work of pulling me out of self-made (and other) predicaments. Great mystery of God! And unveiled every time I get in trouble.

Well, there is nothing like a retreat to help me sift and shift, rearrange and repair the garment called life. And how easy it is for me to see—really see—on a retreat as the waves nuzzle a sandy shore or kiss the sand. It's hard *not* to hear when God speaks from an ocean or over a lake, or on a cool forest path. My hearing is sharper and my eyes clearer when there is less between him and me.

Retreat. It does foster intimacy with my God. My Beloved has found me "still," knowing that he is God![1] He has found me attuned to him, to the peace he offers. Earth-love has its honeymoons, and then it straightens and stretches out into wider and stronger and different vistas of caring. But my years of knowing God do not diminish his passionate pursuit of my heart. Jesus loves me, this I know, for the Bible tells me so.

So, does a breakfast tray in bed really mean anything? It means everything! It is a pampering my woman's soul needs and instinctively wants to enjoy forever. To take my meal in bed and then feed on the Word of God is a fine and a savory thing to do. Aubrey, child of my child, eats literal food with joy but only three times a day. I, child of God, am served *continually* with spiritual food, invited to a perpetual feast with the Lord of lords. It is my whole duty and delight to know God and enjoy him forever!

Prayer

Lord, I want a retreat like this! I need a retreat like this. Where shall I go? When can I go? Make a way out of my personal wilderness, Lord, or I will die of thirst! I need a place to think, a spot where I can talk things over with you and figure out how to slow down my life. I need a private twenty-four hours, Lord, but I'm not sure how to get it. That's where you come in. Show me the way. Meet me there. I can't wait! Amen.

Reflect with Me

- When did I last enjoy a personal retreat?
- How attuned am I to God and the rhythms he wired inside me? How do I gauge that closeness?
- When was the last time I lavishly daydreamed? If I let my-self daydream today, where might my thoughts wander?
- In what specific ways might my loved ones and I benefit if I would arrange some limited kind of personal retreat every month?

Journal Your Feelings

- ☾ The idea of twenty-four hours, or even fewer, to call completely my own makes me feel…
- ☾ The thought of having a leisurely breakfast in bed makes me feel…
- ☾ When I picture myself on a personal retreat, I feel…

Chapter 23

Prayer as a Tryst

Take me away with you! Let's run off together! An elopement with my King-Lover!... Yes! For your love is better than vintage wine.

SONG OF SONGS 1:4, MSG

Prayer. What is it, really? Some people think it's a laundry list of requests recited to the God who can provide. And sometimes it is. Other times it's a thoughtful, handwritten or spoken-aloud communiqué from our heart to his. Prayer can certainly be a gut-wrenching "Help!" from our always-needy and often-inarticulate souls. I have prayed in all of these ways. And God has heard and listened and responded.

Prayer, I think, needs to be demystified. It's a simple

looking up and outward and beyond our circumstances to the One in charge of them. In prayer, our hearts stretch across the chasm of space and build bridges to our Creator. They are the sounds of our souls dressed up in words—or in unintelligible groans and murmurs. Infinity hears, understands, helps. And he does so because he loves.

When we honestly and openly lay our questions and our pain and our praise at the feet of the One who created our inmost parts, we are met with his open-hearted, open-armed love. Because what is prayer if not a tryst with our beloved Groom, the very God in whose image we are made? Books suggest to us how to pray, sermons urge its discipline, and those who pray extol its virtues. And yet many of us shy away from prayer because it seems only an item to be checked off our bloated list of tasks. *O prayer! That you have been so underrated as to be mistaken for a job!* Far from being a task to be completed, prayer is a delicious interlude with the Altogether Lovely One and a meeting he would not miss for the world!

As with communication in any relationship, a dance of sorts happens in the conversation of prayer—back and forth, up and down, now this way, now that—until confidence is established and rapport unwrapped and enjoyed. In my early days of loving God, I often used a kind of baby talk, and I know now he loved that, too. I expressed myself brokenly and in stilted phrases I had learned from others. But he heard me, and he loved me. Then I began to listen to myself talking to God, and I started to know myself for who I was. And, inexplicably, I began to better know who he was.

Later, in the childhood of my faith, our conversations became more involved as I began to tell the whole truth of my mind and heart. In the telling I found relief and help. Other believers identified that as answer to prayer.

Still later, in the adolescence of my relationship with God, I discovered both the joy of using my conversation time with him simply to express my love for him in song and the relief of communicating with tears all that I needed to say. No longer walking into his presence with lowered head and quiet voice, I ran—sometimes joyfully and sometimes desperately—and I threw myself confidently into his arms. I could do that because I had found him to be everything he claimed to be—and more.

Prayer, then, is a conduit to the ruler of the universe, a bridge to the beating heart of the living God. Oh, prayer is not a puzzle. And it is not to be a pain. Neither is it to be a chore or a duty or something to squeeze in only when we're not "too busy." Rather, prayer is a privileged pathway into the inner sanctum, the trysting place of the Creator and his created.

Let the praying begin!

Prayer

You know what, God? I so long to relate to you in easy conversation, but sometimes I forget that doing so is okay, that you want me to talk with you the way I talk with anyone else I love. Oh, not exactly the same way. After all, no listener compares with you. You read my mind and my heart. I'm so grateful that you don't have any rote plan for our times together. And I thank you for welcoming my honesty and my company. That truth astounds me! You in heaven, me on earth, but lovers just the same. O Beloved, can you see me running toward our trysting place? I can't wait to be in your arms. Amen.

Reflect with Me

- Do I plan for private time to converse intimately and honestly with God, or am I "too busy"?
- What do I most want to tell God today?
- What do I most want to ask God today?
- Is something missing in my encounters with God? What might I do to invigorate our love relationship?

Journal Your Feelings

- The thought of setting aside quality conversation time with God makes me feel…
- When I consider prayer as a tryst with my divine Beloved, I feel…
- When I dare to be completely open and honest with God, I feel…

Feast from a Sack Lunch

And my God will meet all your needs according to
his glorious riches in Christ Jesus.
PHILIPPIANS 4:19

He was only a young boy. His goal was never to get his name
in print. He set out from home just to hear a teacher, and his
mom packed his lunch. He was one of thousands listening to
Jesus. As the day wore on, hunger overtook the milling
crowd. The boy touched the pouch at his side. Five pieces of
bread. Two small fish. Enough for him, but that was all.

Moved by the needs of the crowd, Jesus put his finger on
this little lunch and touched it with a miracle. It grew, and it
multiplied. It grew, and it kept growing. In the hands of the
Master, five loaves and two fish were enough for everyone.
Five thousand men—plus women and children—fed and
hungry no more. It wasn't the boy's intent and certainly not

his plan. But he had the lunch, and he gave it to the right person—the only One who could make it enough.

I am amazed and astonished at the power of a small sack lunch in the right hands. And I see things in this story for the too-busy woman—the one who would work and overwork in order to meet her personal needs. I see a boy who took what he had (without trying on his own to make enough for the thousands) and gave it to the only One capable of stretching and multiplying it. It was enough! He didn't insist on "working" to find the needed food or devising schemes he wasn't capable of carrying out to satisfy others. He didn't sit on his pouch and hide it in fear. He knew if he gave it to Jesus, something remarkable would probably happen. And, oh, it did. It *really* did.

God provided a miracle then, and he can surely do so now. Surely none of us needs to trust a paycheck or a raise or a promotion to meet our needs. None of these compares to the faithfulness of our Great Provider. So surely we can work less and devote more of our time and energy to loved ones, neighbors, community, and personal refreshment. After all, who gave the order to work as much as we do? And why do we obey it? Since God has promised to meet all our needs (and I know he does), then why shouldn't we cut back on hours that suck our marrow and drain our joy?

Trying to be our own miracle-working savior will not work. Leaving the miracle work to God might just be a huge relief, a relaxing instead of running. Trusting God to manage our needs might just make room for love and for a life with luster and serendipity. Doing so might just be a risk worth taking.

Show me, young boy, how I can back away from working too much and too long, trying to meet my own needs. Show me how to hand what I have over to Jesus and how to trust him to meet my needs. Tell me it's all right to work a reasonable amount but foolish to think I am my own provider. Remind me that my strength and my wisdom and my resources and my health are limited. Show me the power of placing what I have in the lap of the One who multiplies, the One who feeds us all. And don't let me forget that giving my own "sack lunch" to Jesus might be the most important "work" I ever do.

Prayer

Okay, dear Promise Maker and Keeper, I relinquish my "sack lunch" to you. It's not much, as you know, but you seem to be able and willing to receive and multiply my most meager offerings. Thank you for using children to show me the way. I'm ready to become your child—to let go of my self-reliance and watch, open-eyed, as you work miracles in my life. Multiply, I pray, Lord Jesus! Amen.

Reflect with Me

- How many hours a week do I work for what I want and need? How many years have I been doing this?
- What kinds of things do I think might happen if I cut back on my work hours?
- In what ways have I tried to be my own miracle-working savior? How effective have my efforts been?
- What do I have to offer Jesus, and am I willing to let go of it all? What can I do to place my "sack lunch" in his hands in a tangible way?

Journal Your Feelings

- When I consider that it might truly be possible for me to work less and still have my needs met, I feel...

- Letting Jesus manage what I've always managed makes me feel…
- The thought of living my life as a dependent child on an invisible almighty God makes me feel…

Chapter 25

Enjoying the Small Stuff

However many years a man may live, let him enjoy them all.

ECCLESIASTES 11:8

For whatever reason, root beer tastes better in the summer—especially in a white-frosted mug at a drive-in. Sipped from a can as you're driving along, it's not nearly so sweet. The bottle isn't frosted, and the drink isn't delightful. It isn't much of a treat. But the mug! Ah, the mug. It fits the hand and the heart. It asks us to sit still long enough to relish the feel of the cold glass—long enough to savor the amber elixir.

Root beer! Joy in a mug in the summer! Small thing grown large and measured only by the pleasure it gives.

I know of a man I call the Ecclesiastes man. His name is

Roy. He begins every day with great anticipation and appreciates everything that comes his way. He enjoys his meals—every bite. He enjoys the weather—all kinds. He is thankful for his strength and his health and his God. He is so expert at living gratefully in his todays, he has no room for worrying about tomorrows. Oh yes, this man has discovered the essence of life as did Solomon after all his searching. I know him well because I call him husband.

How does my husband do it? Well, Solomon shows us how. This is the man who tried it all, yet in the richer wisdom of his older years, he came back to the little joys of working, eating, being mindful (fully present) to the world around him, and then lying down to sleep. The simple stuff. The cost-free joys he had missed on his way to the palace.

Some days I chase after the wind just like "prewise" Solomon. I whiz past the little stuff on the way to the big stuff and risk missing much of life's goodness. Who's to say that visiting Disney World is better than planting a rosebush? Who decided that a vacation in Hawaii surpasses a walk in my orchard? By whose enlightened judgment is a flight to the moon more exciting than watching a family of bunnies scamper through a flower garden?

In the book *Little Tree,* I read of a Cherokee Indian who

often took his grandson up the trail in the mountains, and there they sat, for *hours* at a time, watching the animals. They stayed long enough to see a bird gorge on cherries until it couldn't fly. And then they laughed so hard their bellies hurt. They didn't miss the small stuff.

I need to make a concerted effort not to miss the small stuff. I really want to take in each small delight as it presents itself. I want to learn to take as much joy in the colored leaves at my feet as in the fireworks on the Fourth of July.

God's fingerprints are on it all—everything I see. But I tend to overlook the small. Surely, to miss the small stuff— the root beer in the mug, the bird perched in the tree, the mischievous smile on the playful child's face—is to miss the really big stuff, the components that make life a celebration. In order to take notice, I know I need to meander, not jog; stroll, not run; saunter, not speed. It will take *time* to get to really see God's world instead of merely flying through it on our way to that elusive "something better."

Surely I can do better. I can choose, even in the very midst of my busyness, to notice the gigantic joys of little things. And if not now, then soon. As opportunities emerge. And opportunities big and small *will* come, for they are woven into the rhythm of life. Big and small, they are there.

Okay, so when is a root beer *really* a root beer? In an icy mug! In a car! In a drive-in! In the summer! Yes!

$\mathcal{P}$rayer

Father, sometimes I wonder if I have ever really lived a full day. Taking in everything. Not missing the smallest joys and wonders. I remember _____ and _____ from my childhood days and how wonderful they seemed to me then. Help me recapture that childlike delight. Help me fill my heart today by noticing and savoring the small stuff of life. Please don't let me miss the holy fire of the everyday! Amen.

$\mathcal{R}$eflect with $\mathcal{M}$e

- When did I last spend twenty minutes observing or reflecting on the small delights around me?
- What small things bring me joy and refreshment?
- What can I see and fully enjoy from where I'm sitting right now?

◌ What will I do to remind myself to enjoy the small stuff during the week ahead? In what specific ways will I practice being more present in my surroundings?

Journal Your Feelings

◌ When I'm out in nature, I feel…
◌ When I listen to music or read a book or do anything else that feels decadent (because I'm not working), I feel…
◌ When I go for days or weeks or even months without noticing small enjoyments, I feel…

Chapter 26

Appreciating Beauty

He has made everything beautiful in its time. He has also set eternity in the hearts of men; yet they cannot fathom what God has done from beginning to end.

ECCLESIASTES 3:11

We stood in the spacious, light-filled foyer of the Frederik Meijer Gardens and Sculpture Park as the scent of spring strode down the hallway and met us with a smile. It was the middle of a Michigan winter, when we Michiganders get itchy for adventure, and my friend Margo Topp and I had decided to find spring wherever we could. It had definitely arrived at the Gardens.

Knowing that the laundry would still be waiting for us later, we were ready to open winter-weary senses to fully enjoy this experience. We began by strolling into the Spring Room, drawn by the heady smell of lush, purple hyacinths in full bloom. Whereas moments ago we had sloshed through ankle-deep snow and slush, we had suddenly come upon a paradise of sorts. Yellow! Purple! White! Pink! The greenest of green leaves! The primmest of primroses! They all welcomed us with jaunty, smiling faces, and we were overcome with the glory. Here, basking in our admiration, were perfect patches of rainbow-colored petals and happy clusters of daffodils, which wouldn't appear in our yards for months to come. The entire room shouted, "Spring!" It fed our color-hungry eyes with splashes of color, and we savored the sweet, heady scent of the queen of Michigan's seasons.

From there, happily dazed, we wandered into the tropical area, where we were dwarfed and shaded by giant banana trees and even taller bamboo. Creeks gurgled, where outside they were frozen over. Turtles swam and frogs croaked, and tiny finches sang as they hopped from branch to branch. Benches invited us to simply sit and be overcome and overshadowed by the otherworldliness of our tropical environment. A silvery waterfall laughed its way over a precipice and spread exuberant ribbons of water over the shoulders of massive rock outcroppings. A walkway behind the waterfall was mysterious and cozy as we watched the careless water leap with abandon through cracks in the rock.

Margo and I shared an exquisite lunch in an area overlooking the peaceful grounds. Our retreat was complete. In a matter of four short hours, our hearts were enriched and stimulated and filled full once more.

It wasn't as if we had nothing to do. We simply chose not to do it. Margo has five children, a large home, and a husband to care for. I have my own responsibilities. But together we decided to nurture our hearts even on a typically busy, icy day—before our work was finished. And oh, it was so very good! And we were ever so grateful! We had stopped the everyday busyness of life, and we had been struck dumb by the lavish, multicolored extravagance of God's creation. He didn't *have* to make the trees so tall. The tiny finches didn't *have* to have feathers in five brilliant colors to delight our hearts. Orchids and hyacinths didn't *have* to be so utterly beautiful. Creeks could merely water the earth and not curve and crest and crash and undulate over varicolored rocks. We had looked and seen a God whose love for us went so far beyond mere function. He had provided breathtaking beauty as well as providing for our basic needs. The vast, unlimited resources of our God were spilled out for our enjoyment. And we knew we would seek such experiences again and again because this taking time to appreciate beauty is a necessary part of life.

We are created to thrive on the splendor of creation, and that beauty nourishes us in ways we can only begin to understand. Beauty is a need we must not shelve for "someday." After all, Eden may be as close as a backyard or a wide-armed tree or an indoor garden in winter.

Prayer

Lord, I want beauty in my life. I really do. But I need you to help me see how in the world I can make time to go off on field trips in the middle of my busy days. Because right now that seems impossible. And what would people think? I know in my head that shouldn't matter, but please help me to know it in my heart. I do want to understand better—this natural need I have for appreciating the simple beauties of your creation. I'd like to stroll sometimes instead of exercising. I'd like to really behold and inhale the beauty of your world. I'd love to sit by a brook with my arms wrapped around my knees and feast on your natural wonders. What's that? You're delighted to hear this from me? I'm so glad—but I need your help. Please open my mind and some hours in my days simply to appreciate your handiwork. Amen.

Reflect with Me

- When was the last time I experienced the nourishment that comes from appreciating the inspiring splendor of God's creation?
- Where do I habitually run past beauty in my life, past the Eden in my own backyard?
- What activities do I need to eliminate, abbreviate, or postpone in order to enjoy beauty more?
- Where would I most like to go to appreciate beauty? What steps could I take to make that "retreat" a reality?

Journal Your Feelings

- When I see and experience beauty, I feel…
- When I am deprived of beauty, I feel…
- The thought of scheduling time to appreciate beauty makes me feel…

Chapter 27

Choosing to Play

I tell you the truth, unless you change and become like little children, you will never enter the kingdom of heaven.

MATTHEW 18:3

When we're young, it's hard to get too serious about work. We tend to dawdle, procrastinate, fiddle around, eat Cracker Jacks, and become experts at sidestepping anything resembling work. Or…we deftly turn our work into play! Why not?

Work just basically gets in the way of our plans to play. I'm a classic case. As a little girl, when my dad told me to hoe the garden, I was profoundly insulted that he would ask such a thing. I was mad, too. So I cried as I hoed. Then I took a handful of dirt and rubbed it all over my face. I wanted to prove how hard I'd worked, how much I'd perspired, and how dirty I'd become in my labor. Surely his pity would rescue me from further hoeing. It didn't.

When I grew up, I discovered, ironically, how hard it now was to make myself play! Somehow, between childhood and adulthood, play had gotten lost. It was no longer automatic. Work and play switched roles, and I found myself having to make sure I played. As Thomas Kinkade writes in *Lightposts for Living,* it would be so much better if we managed "to acquire the virtues and advantages of maturity without sacrificing the childlike qualities that keep us nearer to joy."

But most of us grownups seem to have sacrificed our childlike qualities, and we wonder why life just isn't fun anymore. The good news is that the very wondering itself can become a vehicle of change if we jump on board the thought and decide to go after some of that wide-eyed wonder we used to enjoy as naturally as we breathed.

No one has ever told me, "You ought to have more fun" or "You really should take a coffee break more often." I have had to do this for myself. All of us need to regenerate ourselves—to play—and it's up to us to give ourselves the time

. Working all the time is neither healthy nor fun. It isn't even all that productive! It may seem risky to have "too much" fun, but it's even a greater risk not to have any! Alexandra Stoddard says it well in *Living Beautifully Together:* "People who take risks, who are creative and love to experiment and improvise, who make the best of what they have, tend to have more fun day to day."

Most women need to start having fun by giving themselves permission to have a playful spirit. Being around someone with a playful spirit helps. The more serious you are, the more you need a friend who makes you laugh—especially at yourself. Another surefire way to lighten up is to watch kids—in a park, a church nursery, your own home. Kids are wonderful, wacky, crazy, mind-boggling, frustrating, and a whole lot of fun. They are the best teachers we will find on our way to recapturing the flag of our childhood. They peer, and they poke, and they feel, and they smell, and they taste. They throw their little hearts into their moments, and life is a virtual playground for them all day long. A little child can lead you back to where life was a gold mine of things to play with: a leaf, a tree, a frog, a blade of grass, a tubful of warm water, bubbles, and a wooden spoon. So simple!

Something else kids do is blend their play into their

work. Work is turned inside out and *becomes* play. What can you do to add a generous portion of play to your work?

Margo and Julie and I decided to try. We met monthly, and each time we brought something to do with our hands while we talked, shared, and prayed together. Julie brought quilt squares to work on. Margo and I made note cards. It was our version of an old-fashioned quilting bee, and the time nourished our souls richly. We called it the Ministry of Hanging Out.

Once, on an impulse, I called my friend Barb Reidburger and said, "Let's iron together on my front porch!" (Typically strange me!) She was astonished, but she laughed, picked up her ironing, and drove over. On my wide, roomy porch with its gorgeous country views, we set up our ironing boards and talked our hearts out while we pressed our clothes. Crazy! Funny! People driving by looked twice. We had a blast.

How can anyone enjoy a life that is nothing but an endless stretch of boring, humdrum, responsible tasks? Most of us women don't need to be told to work. It's what we do. But work can take over our lives and rob us of the joy of play. Breaks are beautiful. Fun is fantastic. Laughter is good medicine. Silliness can be the best response to a world gone sad.

So why not practice taking our play more seriously and

our work a little more lightly? Why not walk through a warm rain, wade barefoot through a puddle, squish mud through your toes, disappear in a hammock, go fishing with a kid, dance to music for fifteen minutes after your workday, jump on your horse, ride a Ferris wheel, play marbles, eat ice cream, go to a ball game, work a puzzle? Why not take off on a bicycle, drive with all the car windows down, play catch with water balloons or raw eggs? Why not toss pebbles in a pond, catch fireflies in a jar, enjoy a candlelit room, and sip a cup of tea without doing anything else at the same time? Why not take a bubble bath, listen to a book on tape, tell ghost stories under a blanket in a darkened room with a bunch of kids?

Why did we stop blowing bubbles and climbing trees and running through sprinklers and jumping rope and doing somersaults in the grass and making angels in the snow? When my grandson Luke was three, he called to me from the trampoline, "C'mon! C'mon and do some flips with me." I gulped and called, "I can't. I'm too old." Thoroughly disgusted, he called back, "Well, just be three!"

Can't we have an ice-cream cone and for once forget about the calories? We might try wearing a playful hat or scarf or earrings—something with a dash of Mad Hatter to it. We could break out a kite on a windy day, try a new food, drive on a new road, be adventurous, curious, unafraid, and open to being surprised and amazed. The possibilities are endless. Just say yes to the little kid inside you. For a bit, refuse to be tyrannized by schedules and responsibilities. After all, you are a child of God. And, like all good dads, he loves to lean over the parapet of heaven and watch you (or join you) at play.

If we can only get little, we may get the idea. If we can stoop to see the world from a child's perspective, we may begin to be wise. If we can let go of our poker-faced grownupness long enough, we may just learn something about the wonderful world of play. Why in the workday world not?

Prayer

Dear God, you designed childhood. And you also never said I had to work my life away. But if I substitute some play for work, I'm afraid of what might happen. You know—the ground I'll lose on the workday treadmill, the money I won't make, the curious and critical stares of other worker bees. I do think I'd be more fun to be around, though. So if

it's really okay with you, I'd like to try playing.
What? You'll come with? Okay, c'mon! Amen.

Reflect with Me

- When was the last time I really played? What did it do for me?
- Have I so habitually sacrificed the child within myself that I don't even know how to play anymore? If so, what can I do about it?
- Do I need to schedule my play in order to make it happen? If so, what will I write on my calendar?
- In what specific way can I blend my work with play and have some fun while I'm being productive?

Journal Your Feelings

- When I'm playing, I feel…
- When I have some playtime to look forward to, I feel…
- When there's no play in my life at all, I feel…

Chapter 28

Spring from a Swing

See! The winter is past; the rains are over and gone.
SONG OF SONGS 2:11

Spring enters, clothed in light, so I stop what I'm doing and take my cup of coffee to the porch swing, feeling a kind of reverence. *Lord, what a wonder you are! I am dumbfounded by the beauty of your seasons and amazed by this debut of yet another magical spring, so mystical and bridelike that it takes my breath away.*

I'm taken aback by the suddenness of spring's arrival, coming so swiftly on the heels of a deep Michigan winter. See there, the gossamer white clouds and the sparkling sun-jewel set in the sky. And there, smell the perfume on the wind. Energy and renewal and starting over are in the air.

Flaming magnolias and jaunty, golden forsythia shout a happy hello to the morning, and the whole earth seems to be stretching upward and outward as it awakens. The confident earth celebrates God's absolute, universal clock by obeying his call to springtime: "Make a joyful noise unto the LORD, all the earth: make a loud noise, and rejoice, and sing praise."[1]

Delicate buds burst from naked tree limbs. Green spears stubbornly poke up through lifeless clumps of last year's lawn. Tractors grumble back and forth across the fields, turning over black loam and pushing seeds deep into the fertile womb of the earth. Orchards are in tight bud, pregnant with the fruit to come. "Let the field be joyful, and all that is therein."[2]

Daffodils and crocuses push stubbornly from their winter cocoons ready to stretch and grow in happy abandon. Frozen waters thaw and flow once more, gurgling with anticipation of the trip ahead and ecstatic at the sights along the way. "Let the rivers clap their hands, let the mountains sing together for joy."[3]

The morning sun cheerily smiles at the waiting world as spring makes its annual debut. It's a sweet and seasonal joy: the voice of all nature giving silent glory to the Creator who thunders his eternal presence through a flower. And we, the earthbound who stand on the hallelujah side of winter, offer glad-hearted adulation and worship at his footstool.

"Exalt the LORD our God and worship at his footstool; he is holy."[4]

Prayer

Lord of the flowers…Lord of the sunshine and Master of springtime…my soul feeds on your glorious handiwork. But all too quickly my heart closes up and goes about its whirling dervish of a day. I miss so much when I don't really look, really see! Spring from a swing. Summer from a beach chair. Fall from a country road. Winter from a windowpane. How long will I continue to miss all you've laid out for my pleasure and inspiration? Open my eyes, Lord. Open my heart. Swing with me. Amen.

Reflect with Me

- ❧ In what ways do I see and hear God in nature?
- ❧ Why do I think God made the earth so magnificent?

- What season is it in my neighborhood right now? When will I take some time to enjoy it? What will I do?
- When was the last time I really saw God's glorious display? How can I do so more often?

Journal Your Feelings

- A stunning sunrise or a dazzling sunset or a delicate flower makes me feel...
- When I connect with God through his creation, I feel...
- When I consider making changes in my life so that I more appreciate the natural splendor around me, I feel...

Chapter 29

More to Life

The meadows are covered with flocks and the val-
leys are mantled with grain; they shout for joy and
sing.

PSALM 65:13

It's summer now, and the woods near my home tremble with
Samson-like strength. It is the puberty of spring bursting
enthusiastically into adolescence. The woods are awash in
fresh color, and vast stretches of violets nonchalantly undress
themselves amid the wet foliage. Friend Sun steals its way
into the heart of this greening tangle, drenching the green-
brown earth with his golden light. I almost cannot work for
the joy of it.

But should I even try? Today, working just might be out

of the question. On this summer Friday, isn't it only right to forsake the usual in order to bask in the incomparable? Oh, the bedazzling joys of this summer day! Surely, to work today would be to ignore the Creator's calling to my soul. To live today as if nothing exquisite had happened to the earth around me would be to walk out on a symphony or scorn a baby's smile or refuse a priceless gift.

While considering my options, I'm happily suspended between earth and sky on my squeaky porch swing while I think about summer. I reflect on how it mothers me, spoiling me with sun, caressing me with cool, blue breezes. At such times I am blissfully sure that things will always be this way: gold sun on leaf, white cloud on sapphire blanket of sky, and warm rain on greening grass. Picnics. Festivals. Hummingbirds. Butterflies. Lightning bugs. And flowers.

Work now? What am I thinking? Summer hasn't danced its way through the doorway of spring for nothing. Besides, I'm hopelessly in love with this season. Doesn't that count for something?

Of all seasons, surely summer is God's best gift to me—a time to reach out for rainbows and gather moonbeams and smile at kittens. And to remember these joys for future replay in another, colder season. Summer is the season of the celebrant, the fulfillment of winter's promises. If I cannot hold summer by the hand today, and if it passes by without my seeing it, what then? Aren't days like this a heaven-sent invitation to worship God in the lavish beauty of his holy creation?

Shimmering rays of sunlight slant their way through the treetops as I decide what to do next. Summer, I think, is God's flamboyant banner of joyous creativity—a purposeful call from heaven to stop and pay attention. To look. To listen to the voice of majesty. And listen I will. Surely, no call to work can be as crucial as this call to worship. For the latter will alter my soul.

Then I know: There will be no work today. There's too much more to life.

Prayer

Father, you prepare a table before me, in the middle of my busyness. You lay out the best silver and the good china. The glasses are crystal. The cloth is a blinding white. You bid me come and dine with you, O Restorer of my soul. And, always

the gracious host, you seat yourself at the head of
the table and wait for me. How could I not stop my
ever-present work and dine with you? God of wonders—that's who you are. I wouldn't miss this time
with you for anything. Praise your holy name!
Amen.

Reflect with Me

- How often do I walk away from work in order to
  spend time with God?
- In what ways do I incorporate worship into my daily
  life? What can I do to make that happen more often?
- When was the last time I played hooky from my usual
  routine? What did I do? How did I feel?
- In what way can I manage my work time differently
  in order to have the freedom to spontaneously answer
  God's gracious invitations?

Journal Your Feelings

- When I deliberately choose to spend valuable time
  (for me) in an unorthodox way, I feel…

- The last time I intentionally spent time with God instead of at work, I felt…
- When I am indulging my senses in my favorite season, I feel…

Chapter 30

Seizing the Day

This is the day the LORD has made; let us rejoice
and be glad in it.

PSALM 118:24

It was a yellow day: sunshiny, warm, and gladly golden. An October sun grinned happily across the lake, saturating the world in a giddy exuberance. Birds sang for no particular reason except their floating happiness, while geese and swans went about their graceful and waterly pursuits.

Despite the first frost, summer flowers still bloomed, and the world stood at respectful attention, drawing in the manifold but fleeting goodness of the day, knowing it would not be thus for long. This amazing day, this gift from God, seemed slipped in, slyly inserted between summer and fall, and I almost could not write for the joy of it. Yet, for the same reason, I could not help but write.

A tug of war began inside. Oh, there was much to be done before winter arrived in earnest. Windows needed to be washed. Seeds had to be gathered from fast-folding garden blossoms. The work was long and waiting for attention. It always would be.

"Want to go for coffee?" The friendly question came, and I quickly glanced at my list…pausing only briefly before saying yes—yes to my husband and to joy and to serendipity. Roy and I drove lazily to a favorite coffee shop in a cozy hamlet beside a river, and we simply sat, drinking in the sun along with our coffee. Sweet blessing, so unexpected! A gilded golden moment on a yellow day. And almost lost to a list.

Movement is slow in the hamlet. Slow and friendly and "how do you do?" People move with measured grace into their shining morning, sharing more than perfunctory hellos with their fellowman. In the coffee shop and on the flower-drenched patio, they touch one another with smiles and words and good-natured well wishing.

A Canada goose rests happily in the shade of a tree at water's edge, taking a break from food gathering, and I ask myself—and want to shout the questions to the world—

How could we not stop? How could any of us not watch? How could we not obey nature's clarion call to our souls? Elegant snowy swans glide past, mirror images of tranquillity. If I were not here, where would I be? At my desk accomplishing, producing? And for what? And for whom? And why? Surely questions worth asking if one is to fully seize a yellow fall day. Or any day.

Later, my husband leaves, and I sit alone on a bench beside the river. The hamlet is full of people, yet I am the only one here on the bench. I am the only one strolling the wild-flower path beside the river. I know winter is coming. Then no one will stroll or sit at the water's edge except in a car. I see the onset of fall in the tumbling, playful clouds and the trees' red-tipped leaves. And I hear the ducks and geese on their way out of town, migrating south.

Each season has its unique beauties and multicolored treasures. But this moment is mine. It is here, and I must seize it now before it is eaten up by tomorrow. So I will not miss this stolen hour in the sun nor care that the windows didn't get washed. My list will not be my master but merely my compass. Having been warmed and nurtured by this glowing morning, I will move more gracefully and gratefully through the hours ahead.

Strange. There are those who say that God does not

speak—or at least not to them. Yet I have stopped for only a short while, and I have heard him—on this yellow day as scarlet leaves dance their way to the welcoming earth. I have heard him in a goose. His words have whispered in the breeze. And beside a river, he spoke.

Prayer

O God, it has been too long since I took even one hour out of my day and set it apart to have coffee with you...to walk and talk with you on a river's edge or on a craggy mountain path or in a crowded café. Surely your voice echoes through the trees and over the waters and in the rain and in the sublime moments of simple days. Make a way for me out of the wilderness of my life, Lord. I'm ready to enter the promised land. Amen.

Reflect with Me

◎ When was the last time I bypassed an unexpected opportunity for time with the Lord in favor of tending to my list? Why?

- How long is my list today? Is it my master or my compass? Why?
- What kind of break rejuvenates me and makes me more grateful and graceful as I move through the rest of the day?
- When can I take an hour's time-out from my work to be warmed and nurtured? What will I do? Where will I go?

Journal Your Feelings

- When I take time-outs, I feel…
- The last time I stopped and made space and time to hear God's voice, I felt…
- When I consider giving myself permission for spontaneous, short, regular getaways from my daily routine, I feel…

On the Path to a Slowed-Down Life

And so you are beginning like one on a journey to a foreign country. You don't yet know the language or the customs of quietness. You feel awkward, out of place, and uneasy on the path to a slowed-down life. But you really want to be here. You're willing to walk through the temporary unease. A ray of light steals in, igniting the hope that your life really can change, that you really do have a voice in how it looks, and that God is more than willing to work with you. You sense, down deep, that a too-busy life is not your only choice.

You've counted the cost of changing and of not changing, and you've made your decision. You've chosen to accept the dare. You've said yes to change. How courageous of you! How pivotal! How worthy—even noble—to begin an unpopular and unfamiliar journey on this road less traveled. You see few footprints ahead of you. Just open space.

And being in such space is an experiment for you at first. But at last you've found a place to enjoy some quiet moments or hours, and you're beginning to breathe more deeply, more slowly, in anticipation. You've stepped away from the ordinary and made room for the extraordinary to occur. You're walking a little straighter and taller—more confidently. You now jangle the keys to some of your prison doors, and you've given yourself permission to use them. You feel willing and able to set out on the road to a freer existence.

What butterfly beauty will emerge as this new season of your life unfolds? It's exciting to think about. You'll find yourself standing back in awe sometimes as you sense yourself blooming, as you recover precious time, as you experience more abiding joy. You'll get away with God and find him to be everything your heart ever yearned for. You'll find it easier and easier to discern the wisest course, so you can add and subtract accordingly. You'll develop spiritual muscles you never knew existed—strengths of heart and character that are essential to staying your chosen path away from busyness. You'll become more fully present to life's cache of golden moments. And you'll discover somewhere along the way that your reclaimed moments have become the most melodious notes of the song called "Your Life."

And so here you are. You welcome this glistening, newborn opportunity to make friends with "doing nothing in particular," and you are ready to celebrate the salutary charms of small solitudes. Keep listening to what your heart is saying. Speak it to the Lord. Listen for his voice in Scripture, nature, and quietness. Gather the courage to reform, reframe, and redesign your life as bits of wisdom come. Record insights and dreams and decisions in a special notebook. Seize moments for the activity of inactivity, for the requirement of rest.

Author Anne Morrow Lindbergh, wife of the famed pilot Charles Lindbergh, reared five children, wrote numerous books, flew with her world-famous husband, and struggled to find solitude enough to nurture her writing spirit. Her river of productivity found its source in her captured times of intentional inactivity. Her classic *Gift from the Sea* was birthed during two weeks of solitude spent in a tiny cabin on a beach. She found her way. You are finding yours. You know that you must if you are not to starve your heart and lose both the essence and the joys of being human.

So congratulate yourself! Celebrate the moment! And do so every chance you get!

Personalize Christ's love: Jesus! He loves me! The Almighty courts my heart! He walks with me. He takes my hand. He promises not to walk away. Love won't. Love can't. And love is the greatest gift of our faithful Savior. I can be confident he will keep wooing my heart and help me remove whatever stands between me and him. It's the job and joy of love. And it's just like Christ, whose love takes the shape of a cross.

Notes

Introduction

1. Galatians 4:15.
2. Galatians 5:1, MSG.
3. Matthew 11:28-30, MSG.

Chapter 1

1. John 15:4-5, MSG.

Chapter 2

1. See Exodus 16:11-35.
2. Luke 11:3, emphasis added.

Chapter 3

1. Genesis 3:5.

Chapter 4

1. Matthew 11:28.

Chapter 5

1. Mark 6:31, MSG.

2. Exodus 20:8, MSG.

3. Exodus 20:11, MSG.

Chapter 7

1. See Genesis 2:15; see Mark 6:31.

2. John 10:10, MSG.

Chapter 10

1. See Galatians 2:20.

Chapter 12

1. John 14:6, KJV.

Chapter 15

1. 1 Corinthians 6:12.

Chapter 17

1. See Genesis 3:6.

Chapter 19

1. Matthew 6:33, emphasis added.

Chapter 21

1. Proverbs 4:25-27.

Chapter 22

1. See Psalm 46:10.

Chapter 28

1. Psalm 98:4, KJV.
2. Psalm 96:12, KJV.
3. Psalm 98:8.
4. Psalm 99:5.

To learn more about WaterBrook Press and view our catalog of products, log on to our Web site:
www.waterbrookpress.com

WATERBROOK
PRESS